GENEALOGIST'S HANDBOOK
FOR ATLANTIC CANADA RESEARCH

GENEALOGIST'S HANDBOOK
FOR ATLANTIC CANADA RESEARCH

Edited by Terrence M. Punch, CG(C)

BOSTON

NEW ENGLAND HISTORIC GENEALOGICAL SOCIETY

Library of Congress Cataloging-in-Publication Data

Genealogist's handbook for Atlantic Canada research / edited by Terrence M.
    Punch
    p. cm.

Includes bibliographical references.
ISBN 0-88082-022-5

1. Atlantic Provinces--Genealogy--Bibliography. 2. Atlantic Provinces--
Genealogy--Handbooks, manuals, etc. 3. Acadians--Atlantic Provinces--
Genealogy--Bibliography. I. Punch, Terrence M. II. New England Historic Gene-
alogical Society.

Z5313.C22A884 1989
[CS88.A88]
929'.1'0720715--dc20   89-12712
                                                                             CIP

CONTENTS

PREFACE

The Genealogist's Handbook for Atlantic Canada Research is intended to be a companion to the similarly named book for research in New England. It is not a methods manual, but a guide to the location of records, repositories and genealogical societies in Atlantic Canada: New Brunswick, Newfoundland and Labrador, Prince Edward Island, and Nova Scotia.

The historical development of each province is not only written in its records; it has determined the very nature of the documentation, its arrangement and its provenance. For example, each province subdivided lands differently for purposes of administration. There are no counties in Newfoundland, because judicial districts and various "bays" are a more useful means of finding both records and the people to which these pertain. The three Maritime Provinces have counties, but their subdivisions vary. New Brunswick's counties contain civil parishes, while Prince Edward Island's counties comprise sixty-seven lots, reflecting grants made in the eighteenth century. In Nova Scotia, "bays," lots and civil parishes mean little, but rural and urban municipalities exist. A short-lived importation of the New England township system graced western Nova Scotia after 1760.

No provincial or municipal registration of vital events was required until the later nineteenth century, so that instead of dealing with town clerks, genealogists find themselves tracking relevant church registers for the necessary information. Likewise, Maritimers were British subjects until 1947, Newfoundlanders until 1949. Thus naturalization files do not exist in the quantity to which American researchers are accustomed. A further difference is that there are few military records for the colonial period, simply because our people joined the British Navy and Army, and their files are in the War Office and Admiralty records of Great Britain.

ARRANGEMENT:

Sections are alphabetical by province and then arranged by record types within each province. The final section covers regional bodies and the Acadians. Reflecting differences between Atlantic Canadian and New England records, the subheadings for each section are as follows:

HISTORICAL OVERVIEW	CEMETERY RECORDS
MAJOR REPOSITORIES	IMMIGRATION RECORDS
VITAL RECORDS	NEWSPAPERS
CENSUS RECORDS	SOCIETIES AND LIBRARIES
LAND RECORDS	PERIODICALS
PROBATE RECORDS	BIBLIOGRAPHY
CHURCH REGISTERS	

ACKNOWLEDGEMENTS

I am grateful to Emery Fanjoy of the Council of Maritime Premiers for the encouragement given to this project, and to Gail Day of his staff for her excellent work in typing and correcting the several draft versions of this handbook. Without their active support this project could not have been completed. Thanks are also due to Robert F. Fellows, CG(C) of the Provincial Archives of New Brunswick for material used to augment the chapter on New Brunswick, and to three staff members of the New England Historic Genealogical Society in Boston, this book's publisher. Gary Boyd Roberts served as overall copy editor; Margaret F. Costello reformatted the text and entered final editorial changes; and Julie Helen Otto prepared for publication the five maps at the beginning of each chapter.

The inspiration for such a cooperative interprovincial venture is the successful Genealogical Institute of the Maritimes. This agency of professional accreditation, the only one in Canada, has supplied the experienced people who have written the several chapters:

New Brunswick - Daniel F. Johnson, CG(C)

Newfoundland and Labrador - Mrs. Elsa H. Hochwald, CG(C)

Nova Scotia - Terrence M. Punch, CG(C)

Prince Edward Island - Miss Orlo L. Jones, CG(C)

Regional Bodies - Stephen A. White, CG(C)

My appreciation to all of them is great.

Terrence M. Punch, CG(C)
Editor

Armdale, Nova Scotia
July 1989

NEW BRUNSWICK

by Daniel F. Johnson, CG(C)

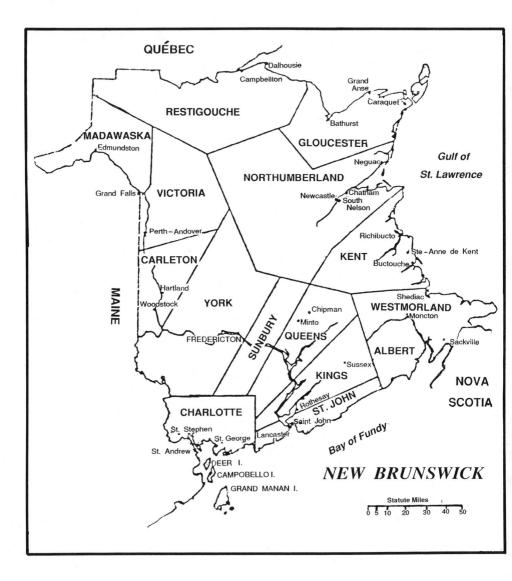

QUÉBEC

Dalhousie
Campbellton

Grand Anse
Caraquet

RESTIGOUCHE

MADAWASKA
Edmundston

Bathurst

GLOUCESTER

Neguac

Gulf of
St. Lawrence

VICTORIA

Grand Falls

NORTHUMBERLAND

Newcastle
Chatham
South Nelson

Perth – Andover

Richibucto
Ste – Anne de Kent

CARLETON

KENT

Buctouche

Hartland

Shediac

Woodstock

YORK

MAINE

Chipman

WESTMORLAND

Moncton

Minto

FREDERICTON

SUNBURY

QUEENS

Sackville

ALBERT

Sussex

KINGS

NOVA

CHARLOTTE

Rothesay
ST. JOHN

SCOTIA

St. Stephen

Lancaster

Saint John

St. George

St. Andrew

Bay of Fundy

DEER I.

CAMPOBELLO I.

NEW BRUNSWICK

GRAND MANAN I.

Statute Miles
0 5 10   20   30   40   50

HISTORICAL OVERVIEW

From the time of its discovery (1604) by Samuel de Champlain until being ceded to the British by the Treaty of Utrecht (1713), New Brunswick with her sister provinces, Nova Scotia and Prince Edward Island, formed the French colony of Acadia. From 1713 to 1755 Britain and France disputed the legal status of the area, a matter that was only resolved following the British seizure of Beauséjour and its associated posts and the removal of much of the Acadian population.

From 1713 (1755) to 1784 the region formed part of the British colony of Nova Scotia under the administration of authorities based in Halifax. The first anglophone settlements of Maugerville, Sackville and Saint John were founded in 1762 by New Englanders, principally by families from Massachusetts and Rhode Island. Some reference to these pre-revolutionary settlements occurs among the records held at the Public Archives of Nova Scotia, 6016 University Avenue, Halifax, N.S. B3H 1W4.

Following the conclusion of the American Revolutionary War, exiled refugees and regiments of the Loyalist corps were transported from New York Harbour to the mouth of the Saint John River. The sudden influx of settlers began the transformation of the former virtual wilderness into a collection of small communities, particularly along the Bay of Fundy coast and up the Saint John River and its tributaries. The Province of New Brunswick was established in June 1784, largely to satisfy the demands of the Loyalists. Also during the late eighteenth century numbers of French-speaking communities developed in northern and eastern coastal regions of New Brunswick. This settlement represented a recovery of the Acadian population as well as the arrival of some Québecois families in the northern districts. Together with the immigration of many Irish into the Miramichi lumbering region and Saint John, these groups account for the most numerous elements in the modern population of the province.

In 1867, New Brunswick, along with Nova Scotia and the two Canadas--Upper and Lower--was a founding province of the Dominion of Canada. A useful text is W.S. MacNutt's *New Brunswick, A History: 1784-1867.* One could also profitably explore library card catalogues for entries under the name of W.O. Raymond, who did considerable work on the early settlement history of the province.

MAJOR REPOSITORIES

Provincial Archives of New Brunswick (P.A.N.B.)

The provincial archives are located on the campus of the University of New Brunswick (mailing address Box 6000, Fredericton, N.B. E3B 5H1). The premises are open daily from Monday through Saturday, 8:30-17:00, except for statutory holidays. There is parking behind the building. The telephone number is 506-453-2122.

Two useful ways of beginning research are to consult *New Brunswick History: A Checklist of Secondary Sources* and its two supplements prepared by Eric L. Swanick in 1974 and 1984, or to check the county guides. If one knows the county within which a family lived, one should obtain from the P.A.N.B. staff a copy of the guide to that specific county, free of charge. In these guides one will find the date each county and parish began, the reel numbers for the relevant census, church, marriage, probate and school records, and the addresses of other institutions that may have useful genealogical resources.

The P.A.N.B. has available for purchase the following census records of the province: Albert County 1851; Carleton County 1851; Charlotte County 1851 (2 vols); Kings County 1851 (2 vols); Saint John County 1851 (2 vols); Westmorland County 1851 (2 vols); York County 1851; Kingston Parish, Kings Co. 1851, 1861, 1871, 1881; Gloucester County 1861; same 1871; Fredericton 1871. In addition, George Hayward, 29 Leeds Dr., Fredericton, N.B. E3B 4S7, has available the census of Sunbury County 1851.

One unusual item in the inventory of the P.A.N.B. is the result of the construction of the Mactaquac Dam some years ago. Part of the project was the removal of people and the subsequent flooding of several communities. Before the inundation took place a team went through all the cemeteries of the area and copied the inscriptions on the headstones of local burying places. These form R.G.173 at the P.A.N.B.

Of use in locating families in the province when the community is not known to the researcher are the provincial directories, the earliest of which dates from 1865/66. There is a Fredericton directory for 1862, and a business directory of Saint John dating back to 1857 with actual city directories starting in 1865. These are held at the P.A.N.B.

The standard genealogical guidebook for the province is Robert Fellows, *Researching Your Ancestors in New Brunswick, Canada*, available from the author, R.R. #1, Mouth of the Keswick, York Co., N.B. E0H 1N0.

VITAL RECORDS

New Brunswick introduced government registration of all vital statistics in 1888, so that the situation changed considerably at that time and the results are reflected in the documentation used by researchers. Birth, marriage and death records for all counties of New Brunswick from 1888 to the present are available only from the *Vital Statistics Branch*, Dept. of Health, Box 6000, Centennial Bldg., Fredericton, N.B. E3B 5H1. Under the present fee structure a payment of $25.00 is required for a search of three years per name for genealogical or historical purposes. These records tend not to be complete until after 1920.

Saint John County Burial Permits, 1889-1919 have been microfilmed and are open to consultation at the P.A.N.B. These records consist of 20,000 burial permits issued by the former Saint John County Board of Health. The 30-volume series normally records the following information: (1) name of deceased, (2) date of death, (3) residence, (4) name of spouse, (5) place of birth, (6) place of death, (7) place of burial, (8) name of physician, (9) name of undertaker, (10) name of father, (11) father's place of birth, (12) name of applicant for permit.

Late Registration of Births, 1810-1887

Such data are based on information supplied to the Vital Statistics Branch by individuals for legal or personal purposes. In many cases, date and place of birth, names of parents and birthplace of father are indicated. These records consist of 25,000 cards arranged alphabetically by the name of the individuals. They may be consulted at the P.A.N.B. on microfilm.

Marriage Registers

These are transcriptions from church records submitted by various denominations. Most entries have been indexed alphabetically by the surname of the groom. Normally each entry contains the name and address of the bride and groom, date of marriage, names of witnesses and of the officiating clergyman or justice of the peace. The P.A.N.B. microfilm contains the following, by county:

Albert	1846-1888	prior to 1846 formed part of Westmorland Co.
Carleton	1832-1888	prior to 1832 formed part of York Co.
Charlotte	1806-1887	
Gloucester	1832-1887	prior to 1826 formed part of Northumberland Co. The years 1860-1872 are missing.
Kent	1826-1887	prior to 1826 formed part of Northumberland Co. The years 1826-1844 are missing.
Kings	1812-1888	
Madawaska		no original marriage registers; one should consult the Pére Henri Langlois Index of 3500 marriages, 1792-1940.
Northumberland	1792-1887	
Queens	1812-1887	
Restigouche	1838-1878	prior to 1838 formed part of Northumberland and Gloucester counties.
Saint John	1819-1887	
Sunbury		registers are missing
Victoria		registers are missing
Westmorland	1790-1887	
York	1812-1888	

Albert 1846-1887 and Westmorland 1790-1856 have been published by Ken Kanner, RR #7, Site 5, Comp. 24, Moncton, N.B. E1C 8Z4. Queens 1812-1861 has been published by Heritage Books Inc., 3602 Maureen Lane, Bowie, MD 20715. Sunbury 1766-1988 has been published by Elizabeth S. Sewell, 54 McKay Dr., Fredericton, N.B. E3A 3S2.

CENSUS RECORDS

The first comprehensive census for New Brunswick was taken in 1851. Since that time enumerations have been taken at ten year intervals. The following census records (microfilm) may be obtained on interlibrary loan only from the National Archives of Canada, 395 Wellington St., Ottawa, Ontario, Canada K1A ON3. Unique in the 1851 Census is the date of entry into New Brunswick. Although some of the 1851 county census records have been published, the remainder are not indexed. Names appear in order of residence visited by the enumerator. Census records include name, age, nativity, religion, occupation, and relationship to head of household. The dates of formation of the several parishes are shown in parentheses after the names of each. For example, Alma parish was created in 1855, but in 1851 the area was within Harvey parish.

ALBERT COUNTY	Prior to 1846 formed part of Westmorland County.				
Alma (1855)	Harvey	1861	1871	1881	1891
Coverdale (1828)	1851	missing	1871	1881	1891
Elgin (1847)	1851	1861	1871	1881	1891
Harvey (1838)	1851	1861	1871	1881	1891
Hillsborough (1786)	1851	1861	1871	1881	1891
Hopewell (1786)	1851	1861	1871	1881	1891

CARLETON COUNTY	Prior to 1832 formed part of York County.				
Aberdeen (1863)	Kent	Kent	1871	1881	1891
Brighton (1830)	1851	1861	1871	1881	1891
Kent (1821)	1851	1861	1871	1881	1891
Northampton (1786)	1851	1861	1871	1881	1891
Peel (1859)	Brighton	1861	1871	1881	1891
Richmond (1853)	Woodstock	1861	1871	1881	1891
Simonds (1842)	1851	1861	1871	1881	1891
Wakefield (1803)	1851	1861	1871	1881	1891
Wicklow (1833)	1851	1861	1871	1881	1891
Wilmot (1867)	Simonds	Simonds	1871	1881	1891
Woodstock (1786)	1851	1861	1871	1881	1891

CHARLOTTE COUNTY	Formed 1786 as an original county.				
Campobello (1803)	1851	1861	1871	1881	1891
Clarendon (1859)	Pennfield & Lepreau		1871	1881	1891

				1881	
Deer Island				1881	
Dufferin (1873)	-----------St. Stephen-----------			1881	1891
Dumbarton (1856)	St. Patrick	1861	1871	1881	1891
Grand Manan (1816)	1851	1861	1871	1881	1891
Lepreau (1859)	Pennfield	1861	1871	1881	1891
Milltown				1881	1891
Pennfield (1786)	1851	1861	1871	1881	1891
Saint Andrews (1786)	1851	1861	1871	1881	1891
Saint Croix (1874)	-----------St. Andrews----------			1881	1891
Saint David (1786)	1851	1861	1871	1881	1891
Saint George (1786)	1851	1861	1871	1881	1891
Saint James (1823)	1851	missing	1871	1881	1891
Saint Patrick (1786)	1851	1861	1871	1881	1891
Saint Stephen (1786)	1851	1861	1871	1881	1891
Upper Mills				1881	1891
West Isles (1786)	1851	1861	1871	1881	1891

GLOUCESTER COUNTY   Prior to 1826 formed part of Northumberland County.

Bathurst (1826)	missing	1861	1871	1881	1891
Beresford (1814)	missing	1861	1871	1881	1891
Caraquet (1831)	missing	1861	1871	1881	1891
Inkerman (1855)	missing	1861	1871	1881	1891
New Bandon (1831)	missing	1861	1871	1881	1891
Saumarez (1814)	missing	1861	1871	1881	1891
Shippegan (1851)	missing	1861	1871	1881	1891
St. Isidore (1881)	---------Saumarez & Inkerman----------				1891

KENT COUNTY   Prior to 1826 formed part of Northumberland County.

Acadiaville (1876)	missing	-----Carleton-----		1881	1891
Carleton (1814)	missing	1861	1871	1881	1891
Dundas (1826)	missing	1861	1871	1881	1891
Harcourt (1826)	missing	1861	1871	1881	1891
Huskisson (1826)	missing	missing	1871	1881	
Palmerston (1855-66)	missing	1861	--------St. Louis-------		
Richibucto (1826)	missing	1861	1871	1881	1891
Saint Louis (1866)	missing	Palmerston	1871	1881	1891
Saint Mary (1867)	missing	Wellington	1871	1881	1891
Saint Paul (1883)	---------Saint Mary & Harcourt---------				1891
Weldford (1835)	missing	1861	1871	1881	1891
Wellington (1814)	missing	1861	1871	1881	1891

KINGS COUNTY	Formed 1786 as an original county.				
Cardwell (1874)	Sussex	Sussex	Sussex	1881	1891
Greenwich (1795)	1851	1861	1871	1881	1891
Hammond (1858)	Upham	1861	1871	1881	1891
Hampton (1795)	1851	1861	1871	1881	1891
Havelock (1858)	Studholm	1861	1871	1881	1891
Kars (1859)	Kingston	missing	1871	1881	1891
Kingston (1786)	1851	1861	1871	1881	1891
Norton (1795)	1851	1861	1871	1881	1891
Rothesay (1870)	Hampton	Hampton	1871	1881	1891
Springfield (1786)	1851	1861	1871	1881	1891
Studholm (1840)	1851	missing	1871	1881	1891
Sussex (1786)	1851	1861	1871	1881	1891
Upham (1835)	1851	1861	1871	1881	1891
Waterford (1874)	Sussex	Sussex	Sussex	1881	1891
Westfield (1786)	1851	1861	1871	1881	1891

MADAWASKA COUNTY	Prior to 1832 formed part of York County. From 1832 to 1850 formed part of Carleton Co. From 1850 to 1873 formed part of Victoria Co.				
Madawaska (1833)	1851	1861	1871	1881	1891
Sainte Anne (1877)	----St. Léonard & St. Basile----			1881	1891
Saint Basile (1850)	1851	1861	1871	1881	1891
Saint François (1877)	1851	1861	1871	1881	1891
Saint Hilaire (1877)	-----------Madawaska-----------			1881	1891
Saint Jacques (1877)	-----------Madawaska-----------			1881	1891
Saint Léonard (1850)	1851	1861	1871	1881	1891

NORTHUMBERLAND COUNTY	Formed 1786 as an original county.				
Alnwick (1786)	1851	1861	1871	1881	1891
Blackville (1830)	1851	1861	1871	1881	1891
Blissfield (1830)	1851	1861	1871	1881	1891
Chatham (1814)	1851	1861	1871	1881	1891
Derby (1859)	Nelson	1861	1871	1881	1891
Glenelg (1814)	1851	1861	1871	1881	1891
Hardwicke (1815)	Glenelg	1861	1871	1881	1891
Ludlow (1814)	1851	1861	1871	1881	1891
Nelson (1814)	1851	1861	1871	1881	1891
Newcastle (1786)	1851	1861	1871	1881	1891

Northesk (1814)	1851	1861	1871	1881	1891
Rogersville (1881)	Nelson	Nelson	Nelson	Nelson	1891
Southesk (1879)	--------------Northesk-------------			1881	1891

QUEENS COUNTY Formed 1786 as an original county.

Brunswick (1816)	missing	1861	1871	1881	1891
Cambridge (1852)	missing	1861	1871	1881	1891
Canning (1827)	missing	1861	1871	1881	1891
Chipman (1835)	missing	1861	1871	1881	1891
Gagetown (1786)	missing	missing	1871	1881	1891
Hampstead (1786)	missing	1861	1871	1881	1891
Johnston (1839)	missing	1861	1871	1881	1891
Petersville (1838)	missing	1861	1871	1881	1891
Waterborough (1786)	missing	1861	1871	1881	1891
Wickham (1786)	partial	1861	1871	1881	1891

RESTIGOUCHE COUNTY Prior to 1827 formed part of Northumberland County. From 1827 to 1838 formed part of Gloucester County.

Addington (1826)	1851	1861	1871	1881	1891
Colborne (1839)	1851	1861	1871	1881	1891
Dalhousie (1839)	1851	1861	1871	1881	1891
Durham (1839)	1851	1861	1871	1881	1891
Eldon (1826)	1851	1861	1871	1881	1891

SAINT JOHN COUNTY (City Wards)

* The 1851 Census contains an unidentified area thought to be a sector of Saint John City.

Albert	missing	1861	1871	1881	1891
Brooks	missing	missing	1871	1881	1891
Dufferin					1891
Duke	1851	missing	1871	1881	1891
Guy	missing	missing	1871	1881	1891
Kings	1851	missing	1871	1881	1891
Lansdowne	missing	missing	--Portland---		1891
Lorne	missing	missing	--Portland---		1891
Prince	missing	missing	1871	1881	1891
Queens	1851	missing	1871	1881	1891
Stanley	missing	missing	--Portland---		1891

Sydney	1851	missing	1871	1881	1891
Victoria	missing	missing	--Portland---		1891
Wellington	missing	missing	1871	1881	1891

SAINT JOHN COUNTY (Parishes) Formed 1786 as an original county.

Lancaster (1786)	missing	missing	1871	1881	1891
Musquash (1877)	missing	missing	Lancaster	1881	1891
Portland (1786-1889)	missing	missing	partial	1881	
Saint Martin (1786)	partial	missing	1871	1881	1891
Simonds (1839)	1851	missing	1871	1881	1891

SUNBURY COUNTY Formed 1786 as an original county.

Blissville (1834)	1851	1861	1871	1881	1891
Burton (1786)	1851	1861	1871	1881	1891
Gladstone (1874)	-------------Blissville-------------			1881	1891
Lincoln (1786)	1851	1861	1871	1881	1891
Maugerville (1786)	1851	1861	1871	1881	1891
Northfield (1857)	Sheffield	1861	1871	1881	1891
Sheffield (1786)	1851	1861	1871	1881	1891

VICTORIA COUNTY Prior to 1832 formed part of York County. From 1832 to 1850 formed part of Carleton County.

Andover (1833)	1851	1861	1871	1881	1891
Drummond (1872)	Andover	---Grand Falls--		1881	1891
Gordon (1863)	Perth	Perth	1871	1881	1891
Grand Falls (1852)	Andover	1861	1871	1881	1891
Lorne (1871)	Perth	Perth	Perth	1881	1891
Perth (1833)	1851	1861	1871	1881	1891

WESTMORLAND COUNTY Formed 1786 as an original county.

Botsford (1805)	1851	1861	1871	1881	1891
Dorchester (1787)	1851	1861	1871	1881	1891
Moncton (parish) (1786)	1851	1861	1871	1881	1891
Moncton (town)	missing	1861	missing	1881	1891
Sackville (1786)	1851	1861	1871	1881	1891
Salisbury (1786)	1851	1861	1871	1881	1891
Shediac (1827)	1851	1861	1871	1881	1891
Westmorland (1786)	1851	1861	1871	1881	1891

YORK COUNTY   Formed 1786 as an original county.

Bright (1869)	Queensbury & Douglas 1871		1881	1891
Canterbury (1855)	Douglas	1861	1871	1881	1891
Douglas (1824)	1851	1861	1871	1881	1891
Dumfries (1833)	1851	1861	1871	1881	1891
Fredericton (1786)	1851	1861	1871	1881	1891
Kingsclear (1786)	1851	1861	1871	1881	1891
Manners Sutton (1857)	Kingsclear	1861	1871	1881	1891
Marysville	----------------Saint Marys----------------				1891
New Maryland (1846)	missing	1861	1871	1881	1891
North Lake (1879)	------------------Dumfries------------------				1891
Prince William (1786)	missing	1861	1871	1881	1891
Queensbury (1786)	1851	1861	1871	1881	1891
Saint Marys (1786)	1851	1861	1871	1881	1891
Southampton (1833)	missing	1861	1871	1881	1891
Stanley (1846)	1851	1861	1871	1881	1891

LAND RECORDS

Land Petitions 1784-1850 P.A.N.B. (Microfilm)

To facilitate the settlement of Loyalist refugees, tracts of land were surveyed and partitioned into grant lots. Some lands were granted to Loyalist regiments lately disbanded in New Brunswick. However, most refugees acquired individual lots of 100 or 200 acres. In later years, land grants were a tool of government policies to encourage settlement in the Province as well as bounty for military service in the regular British forces. Early settlers often inhabited vacant properties while awaiting legal ownership. As land was cleared and cultivated, applications or memorials were submitted requesting that a grant be issued. Since there was no set format, many petitions are rich in biographical detail. There are associated papers concerning disputes in ownership. The 50,000 petitions have been sorted firstly by year and secondly by name of memorialist.

Land Grants 1763-1868 P.A.N.B. (Microfilm)

By the terms of each grant, settlers were required to clear and cultivate a specified number of acres, and to erect a cabin of certain dimensions within a set time period, normally three years. Land Grants during this period were subsequently illustrated in Cadastral Maps. When the conditions of the grant were not met, the land was escheated. Land Grants contain precise property descriptions indicating boundary lines. (See Hannay's Index 1765-1900 Micro F277).

Registry Office Records 1784-Present P.A.N.B. (Microfilm)

Property titles may be searched through the registry office records. These contain deeds, mortgages, leases, liens and (occasionally) wills. The original books remain at the court house in each county seat. Microfilmed copies for most counties may be viewed at the P.A.N.B., University of New Brunswick Campus, Fredericton, N.B. Indices are arranged by time periods and indexed by names of grantor and grantee.

PROBATE RECORDS

Probate records for most counties are deposited at the P.A.N.B. The probate files and books for Albert and Westmorland counties are in the custody of the Registrar of Probate, Box 5001, Moncton, N.B. E1C 8R3. Wills, petitions for probate, letters of administration, inventories of estates and miscellaneous affidavits are found here. Many counties have probate files and probate books. Probate records for Kent County were destroyed by fire.

County   (**F** Files **B** Books **O** Originals **M** Microfilm)

County			County		
Albert	B M	1845-1904	Queens	F M	1785-1885
				F O	1886-1950
				B M	1788-1891
Carleton	F O	1833-1956	Restigouche	F O	1895-1968
	B M	1833-1956		B M	1839-1895
Charlotte	F M	1785-1885	Saint John	F O	1785-1963
	F O	1886-1951		B M	1785-1904
	B M	1800-1965		B O	1888-1963
Gloucester	F M	1836-1885	Sunbury	F O	1786-1968
	F O	1886-1956		B M	1786-1885
	B O	1926-1950		B O	1886-1968
Kings	F O	1786-1949	Victoria	F O	1845-1956
	B M	1787-1885		B M	1850-1885
	B O	1886-1965		B O	1886-1927
Madawaska	F O	1894-1949	Westmorland	B M	1787-1885
	B O	1909-1930			
North-	F O	1860-1966	York	F O	1786-1958
umberland	B O	1870-1871		B M	1794-1887
	B M	1872-1885		B O	1888-1953
	B O	1886-1970			

CHURCH RECORDS

The largest single collection of microfilmed church records, including vestry minutes, baptisms, marriages and burials, is housed at the P.A.N.B., Fredericton. Many reels are confidential and the permission of the local clergyman may be required. The listing below is a selection of registers that are open to use, and which open at a date prior to 1888 (the year that government records of vital statistics begins). Researchers should be aware that this list contains some, but not all, church records, as many have not been microfilmed. (A Anglican; B Baptist; C Catholic; Cong Congregationalist; D Disciples of Christ; M Methodist; P Presbyterian; U United)

Albert County:	Elgin Circuit	M/U	1876-1948
	Hopewell	A	1884-1959
Carleton County:	Northumberland	A	1791-1970
		M/U	1868-1966
	Richmond	P	1883-1961
	Woodstock	A	1791-1970
		P	1858-1882
		U	1849-1971
Charlotte County:	Campobello	A	1830-1970
	Fairhaven	B	1868-1927
	Grand Harbour	B	1862-1970
	Grand Manan	A	1832-1962
		M	1885-1899
	Leonardville	D	1858-1912
	Lepreau	A	1861-1970
	Milltown	M/U	1850-1966
	Oak Bay	A	1815-1849
		U	1856-1910
	Oak Hill	U	1878-1964
	Pennfield	A	1822-1901
		B	1853-1944
	Rollingdam	P	1846-1887
	St. Andrews	A	1787-1961
		P	1824-1970
		M	1837-1874
	St. George	A	1822-1900
		B	1839-1928
	St. Patrick	P	1823-1887
	St. Stephen	M/U	1794-1943
		Cong	1847-1921
		A	1812-1945 (Christchurch)

	St. Stephen	A	1870-1915 (Trinity)
	Second Falls	B	1871-1923
	Tower Hill	P	1874-1959
	Waweig	P	1856-1953
	Whittiers Bridge	P/U	1846-1887
Gloucester County:	Bathurst	A	1864-1970
		C	1798-1920 (Sainte-Famille)
		C	1881-1920 (Cathedral)
		M	1832-1900
		P	1858-1918
	Belledune	C	1836-1920
	Caraquet	C	1768-1920
	Inkerman	C	1818-1920
	Lemeque	C	1840-1920
	Paquetville	C	1874-1920
	Petit Rocher	C	1824-1920
	Pokemouche	C	1843-1920
	Robertville	C	1885-1920
	St. Isidore	C	1876-1920
	Shippegan	C	1824-1920
	Tracadie	C	1798-1920
Kent County:	Baie-des-Verts	A	1801-1870
	Buctouche/Richibucto	A	1829-1956
	St. Louis de Kent	C	1800-1870
	Weldford	A	1848-1955
	Wellington	A	1870-1898
Kings County:	Dutch Valley/ Hammond	A	1873-1884
	Greenwich	A	1801-1953
	Hammond River	P	1880-1902 (with Salt Springs)
	Hampton	A	1819-1970
		M	1876-1901
		U	1882-1925
	Kingston	A	1816-1970
		M	1862-1910
	Norton	A	1817-1956
	Rothesay	A	1870-1969
	Studholme/Sussex	A	1817-1956
	Sussex	U	1857-1970
	Upham	A	1848-1963
	Westfield	A	1801-1953

Madawaska County:	Edmundston	P/U	1898-1970
		C	1869-1920 (St.-Hilaire)
		C	1872-1920 (Ste.-Anne)
	Notre-Dame	C	1880-1920
	Saint-Basile	C	1792-1920
	Saint Francis	C	1859-1920
	Saint-Jacques	C	1880-1920
	St. Leonard	C	1854-1921
Northumberland County:	Boiestown	U	1872-1976
	Chatham	M/P/U	1817-1971
		A	1822-1923
	Miramichi/Nelson	C	1801-1858 (with Bartibog)
	Nequac	C	1798-1920
	Newcastle	P	1830-1927
		A	1843-1970
		M	1882-1961
	Red Brook Indian Reservation		1842-1900
	Whitneyville	B	1819-1917
Queens County:	Cambridge	A	1883-1958
	Canning	A	1846-1914
		B	1850-1873
	Chipman	A	1846-1914
	Cody's	B	1832-1960
	Coles Island	B	1886-1971
	Gagetown	A	1786-1958
		M	1859-1910
		U	1861-1970
	Lower Cambridge	B	1839-1972
	McDonald's Corner	B	1823-1972
	Narrows East	B	1856-1964
	New Jerusalem	B	1838-1881
		U	1858-1953
	Petersville	A	1846-1958
	Scotchtown	B	1856-1911
	Thornetown	B	1840-1918
	Welsford	U	1873-1966
	White's Cove	B	1845-1971
Restigouche County:	Campbelltown	P/U	1874-1965
	Charlo	C	1853-1920
	Dalhousie	C	1843-1920

	Jacquet River	C	1886-1920
	Nash Creek	C	1867-1920
	New Carlisle	A	1820-1904
	New Mills	P/U	1887-1971
	Sainte-Anne	C	1759-1795
Saint John City:	Old Stone Church	A	1852-1970
	St. George's	A	1826-1972
	Trinity	A	1836-1957
	Immaculate Conception	C	1821-1973
	Carmarthen St.	M	1879-1957
	St. John's	P	1844-1951
	St. Stephen's	P	1866-1935 (with Knox)
	Calvin	P/U	1855-1918
	St. Andrew's	P/U	1817-1961 (with St. David's)
	West Side Kirk	P/U	1857-1971
	Centenary	U	1839-1973 (Queen Square)
	Exmouth Street	U	1852-1973
Saint John County:	Carleton	M	1884-1972
		U	1854-1972
	Lancaster	A	1874-1912
	Musquash	C	1861-1970 (St. Ann's)
	St. Martins	A	1876-1930
	Simonds	A	1846-1907
Sunbury County:	Fredericton Jct.	B	1875-1976
	Lincoln	B	1833-1923
	Maugerville	A	1787-1878
	Oromocto	C	1866-1958
	Sheffield	M/U	1835-1971
		M	1874-1905
Victoria County:	Andover	A	1845-1970
		U	1845-1945
		P/U	1848-1945
	Grand Falls	C	1868-1920
		A	1882-1941
	Kincardine	M	1835-1906
		P	1870-1970
	Maliseet	C	1870-1920
Westmorland County:	Barachois	A	1812-1870
	Botsford	A	1839-1853 (with Cape Tormentine)

	Dundas	A	1870-1898
	Memramcook	A	1806-1870
	Moncton	A	1843-1870 (St. George's)
		U	1856-1970 (St. John's)
		U	1876-1971 (St. James)
	Saint-Anselme	A	1832-1870
	Scoudouc	C	1850-1870
	Shediac	A	1822-1881 (St. Martin's)
		A	1829-1857 (St. Andrew's)
	Sackville	M/U	1839-1958
	Shemoque	C	1813-1899
York County:	Bright	A	1845-1934
	Canterbury	M	1883-1961
	Douglas	A	1843-1928
	Fredericton	A	1816-1959 (Christchurch)
		A	1843-1887 (St. Mary's)
		C	1825-1870 (St. Dunstan's)
		P/U	1833-1971 (St. Paul's)
		U	1794-1971 (Wilmot)
	Harvey Station	U	1855-1945
	Kingsclear	A	1816-1955
		B	1825-1966
	Mactaquack	B	1844-1972
	New Maryland	A	1836-1883
	Prince William	U	1854-1971
		P	1877-1977
		A	1791-1970 (with Queensbury)
	Taymouth	U	1843-1966

Researchers are advised to contact the P.A.N.B. to learn whether the records of other churches are held there in microform. Those planning to travel to New Brunswick to consult such film are advised to write well in advance to the relevant clergyman for permission to view restricted microfilmed church records. Those pursuing research into Anglican families could establish contact by writing to the Diocesan Archives, 116 Princess St., Saint John, N.B. E2L 1K4. Inquiries regarding Catholic records should be made to the Diocesan Archives, One Bayard Dr., Saint John, N.B. E2L 3L5.

CEMETERY RECORDS

Cemetery records are found only in the larger municipalities such as Saint John. Records such as Fernhill or Cedar Hill Cemetery are maintained by private companies. In rural areas, one must rely on local church burial registers, newspaper obituaries and epitaph transcriptions.

Epitaph projects have been initiated by individuals or local church, genealogical and historical organizations. The P.A.N.B. has acquired copies of many, but not all, of these works. The researcher is advised to contact a local library organization. *Generations*, the newsletter of the New Brunswick Genealogical Society, is another valuable source of headstone transcriptions. G.F. Somerville, 84 Beach Cres., Saint John, N.B. E2K 2E4, has produced *Some Burial Records of the Loyalist Burial Ground, Saint John*, and Lennox Bagnell, 330 Prince St., Saint John, N.B. E2M 1P5, published *Burial Records of the Church of England Cemetery, Saint John, N.B.*

IMMIGRATION

The Custom House Records, on microfilm at the P.A.N.B., include passenger lists, manifests, etc., of ships arriving at the Port of Saint John in 1833, 1834, 1837, 1838, containing over 10,000 names. A book, *Passengers to New Brunswick: The Custom House Records*, covers this material. It is available from the Saint John Branch of the New Brunswick Genealogical Society, Box 3813, Station "B", Saint John, N.B. E2M 5C2.

The alms house records of Saint John are registers containing the names of inmates, their ages, religion, dates of admission and discharge, and place of origin. Permission of the provincial archivist is required for use of these records after 1910. The records after 1850 are held at the P.A.N.B., while the originals for 1845-1850 are kept at the New Brunswick Museum in Saint John. The book, *Saint John County Alms & Work House 1845-1850*, is available from D.F. Johnson, Box 2387, Saint John, N.B. E2L 3V6.

NEWSPAPERS

The single largest repository of newspapers is in the Harriet Irving Library, Box 7500, University of New Brunswick Campus, Fredericton, N.B. E3B 5H5. The Vital Statistics Committee of the New Brunswick Genealogical Society began to extract all birth, marriage and death information from all New Brunswick newspapers. Five volumes were published, encompassing 1784-1834. The project has been continued by D.F. Johnson on a private basis. To date twenty-two volumes have been published to cover the period to 1865.

To learn about the existence of newspapers in relevant areas, one should consult J. Russell Harper, *Historical Directory of New Brunswick Newspapers* (Fredericton, 1961). Some early newspapers include, from Saint John, the *(Royal) St. John Gazette* (1784), *New Brunswick Royal Gazette* (1785; after 1815 in Fredericton), the *Times or True Briton*, the *City Gazette & General Advertiser*, *New Brunswick Courier*, *The Star*, and *New Brunswick Chronicle*, all before 1830. There were also the *Fredericton Telegraph*, the *Miramichi Mercury*, the *Saint Andrews Herald*, the *Saint Andrews Courant*, the *Saint Andrews Standard*, and the *Gleaner & Northumberland Schediasma*, all before 1834. The *Union List of Newspapers Held by Canadian Libraries* (National Library of Canada, 1983), provides a more specific listing of newspapers.

SOCIETIES & LIBRARIES

New Brunswick Genealogical Society (N.B.G.S.)
Box 3235, Station B,
Fredericton, N.B.
E3A 5G9

publishes quarterly *Generations* newsletter, and is composed of representatives from branch societies:

Boiestown Branch, N.B.G.S.	c/o Wilmot Ross, R.R. #1 Nashwaak Bridge, N.B. E0H 1R0
Capital Branch, N.B.G.S.	c/o Mrs. Eleanor Allen Comp. 26, Site 18, R.R. #10 Fredericton, N.B. E3B 6H6
Carleton County Branch, N.B.G.S.	c/o John R. Glass Box 125, Clark St. Hartland, N.B. E0J 1N0
Grand Manan Branch, N.B.G.S.	c/o Mrs. Gleneta Hettrick Grand Harbour Grand Manan, N.B. E0G 1X0
Restigouche Branch, N.B.G.S.	c/o Jackson B. Ross 6 Chaleur St. Campbelltown, N.B. E3N 1T1

Saint John Branch, N.B.G.S.

Box 3813, Station B
Saint John, N.B.
E2M 5C2

Southeastern Branch, N.B.G.S.

c/o Wayne Gilcash, R.R. #1
College Bridge, N.B.
E0A 1L0

Much useful local information may be obtained by consulting the holdings of libraries, historical societies and museums. A selection of active institutions in New Brunswick is offered here, but the list is by no means exhaustive.

Albert-Westmorland-Kent Regional Library
Box 708
Moncton, N.B.
E1C 8M9

Bibliothéque Regionale du haut Saint-Jean
50 rue Queen
Edmundston, N.B.
E3V 3N4

Carleton County Historical Society
Box 898
Woodstock, N.B.
E0J 2B0

Central Miramichi Historical Society
Box 38
Doaktown, N.B.
E0C 1G0

Chaleur Regional Library
Box 607
Campbelltown, N.B.
E3N 3H1

Charlotte County Historical Society
78 Prince William St.
St. Stephen, N.B.
E3L 1S3

Genealogical Library, Church of Latter Day Saints
Box 414
Hampton, N.B.
E0G 1Z0

Grand Falls Museum
Box 1572
Grand Falls, N.B.
E0J 1M0

Grand Manan Historical Society
Grand Harbour, N.B.
E0G 3B0

Kings County Historical Society
Centennial Bldg.
Hampton, N.B.
E0G 1Z0

Legislative Library
Box 6000
Fredericton, N.B.
E3B 5H1

Library & Archives Division
New Brunswick Museum
277 Douglas Ave.
Saint John, N.B.
E2L 1E5

L.P. Fisher Public Library
Box 1540
Woodstock, N.B.
E0J 2B0

Lutz Mountain Heritage Museum
Box 2952
Station "A"
Moncton, N.B.
E1C 8T8

Moncton Museum
20 Mountain Rd.
Moncton, N.B.
E1C 2J8

Old Manse Public Library
225 Mary St.
Newcastle, N.B.
E1V 1Z3

Perth-Andover Public Library
Box 128
Perth-Andover, N.B.
E0J 1V0

Quaco Museum and Library
St. Martins, N.B.
E0G 2Z0

Queens County Museum
Tilley House
Gagetown, N.B.
E0G 1V0

Ralph Pickard Bell Library
Mount Allison University
Sackville, N.B.
E0K 1B0

Restigouche Regional Museum
Box 1717
Dalhousie, N.B.
E0K 1B0

Ross Memorial Library
Box 250
St. Andrews, N.B.
B0G 2X0

St. Croix Public Library
1 Budd Avenue
St. Stephen, N.B.
E3L 1E8

Saint John Regional Library
One Market Square
Saint John, N.B.
E2L 4Z6

St. Michael's Historical Museum
Box 368
Chatham, N.B.
E1N 3A7

Société Historique Acadienne
C.P. 2363, Station "A"
Moncton, N.B.
E1C 8J3

Société Historique du Comté de Restigouche
C.P. 534
Campbelltown, N.B.
E3N 3G9

Société Historique de Kent
C.P. 697
Bouctouche, N.B.
E0A 1G0

Société Historique du Madawaska
C.P. 474
Edmundston, N.B.
E3B 3L1

Sunbury West Historical Society
Fredericton Junction, N.B.
E0G 1T0

United Empire Loyalists Association
Fredericton Branch
54 MacKay Drive
Fredericton, N.B.
E3A 3S2

York Regional Library
4 Carleton St.
Fredericton, N.B.
E3B 5P4

York-Sunbury Historical Museum
Box 1312
Fredericton, N.B.
E3B 5C8

BIBLIOGRAPHY

Bell, D.G. *Early Loyalist Saint John.* Fredericton, 1983.

Dubeau, Sharon. *New Brunswick Loyalists.* Agincourt, Ont., 1983.

Fellows, Robert. *Researching Your Ancestors in New Brunswick, Canada.* Fredericton, 1979.

Hannay, James. *History of New Brunswick.* Saint John, 1909.

MacNutt, W.S. *New Brunswick, a History: 1784-1967.* Toronto, 1963.

Maxwell, Lilian. *An Outline of the History of Central New Brunswick.* Sackville, N.B., 1937.

Raymond, W.O. *The River St. John*, ed. J.C. Webster. Sackville, N.B., 1950.

Rigby, A.C. *A guide to the manuscript collections in the Provincial Archives of New Brunswick.* Fredericton, 1977.

Taylor, Hugh. *New Brunswick History: A Checklist of Secondary Sources.* Fredericton, 1975.

Wright, Esther C. *The Loyalists of New Brunswick.* Fredericton, 1955.

NEWFOUNDLAND AND LABRADOR

by Elsa H. Hochwald, CG(C)

NEWFOUNDLAND
AND
LABRADOR

1 Bonavista
2 Carbonear
3 Catalina
4 Corner Brook
5 Cupids
6 Ferryland
7 Fogo
8 Fortune
9 Gander
10 Goose Bay
11 Grand Falls
12 Happy Valley
13 Harbour Grace
14 Holyrood
15 Labrador City
16 L'Anse-Aux-Meadows
17 Placentia
18 Port-au-Choix
19 Port-Aux-Basques
20 St. Anthony
21 Stephenville
22 St. John's
23 Trinity
24 Twillingate
25 Wabush

LABRADOR

ATLANTIC OCEAN

STRAIT OF BELLE ISLE

White Bay

Notre Dame Bay

Bonavista Bay

NEWFOUNDLAND

GULF OF ST. LAWRENCE

Fortune Bay

Placentia Bay

HISTORICAL OVERVIEW

The history of the island of Newfoundland has been shaped as much by its strategic position of stepping stone between Europe and America as by the fishing banks off its rocky coast. Newfoundland is claimed as one of the New World's earliest places of European settlement. The earliest documentary evidence of visits to the island is found in the Vinland Sagas. About the year 1000 the Viking, Leif Eriksson, chanced upon Vinland. The actual location of the Viking expeditions to the North American Atlantic coast has been hotly contested. The discovery of Viking ruins on the northern tip of the island of Newfoundland at L'Anse aux Meadows confirms that there were, about 1000 A.D., Vikings who remained there sufficiently long to establish a village.

The island of Newfoundland is about 43,000 square miles of barren interior and deep bays. The coastline is about 6,500 miles long, but from the time of the Viking voyages it is five hundred years before we find the next records of European habitation -- the Basques who set up whaling stations (at least ten) between about 1540 and 1610.

On 24 June 1497 John Cabot sighted and claimed Newfoundland for England. In 1502 Miguel Corte-Real was granted title to Newfoundland by King Manöel of Portugal. Cabot and Corte-Real were simply claiming land which was habitually visited during the summers by those involved in supplying fish for the European market. The growing populations of Europe increased the value and demand for fish, particularly in the Roman Catholic countries. In 1527 John Rut, an Englishman, visited St. John's Harbour, where he counted fourteen ships from Brittany, Normandy and Portugal.

In 1583 Humphrey Gilbert entered St. John's Harbour and formally took possession of the island for the Crown. Thus Newfoundland became England's first colony. Gilbert proclaimed a code of law, part of which permitted the practice of only one religion, the Anglican faith of the Church of England. From 1583 until 1824 Newfoundland was considered part of the British Empire, but only in the latter years was it given official colonial status. Settlement developed slowly, due largely to mercantile policy favouring seasonal fishery. In the early 1600s many attempts were made to establish plantations, beginning with John Guy's post in 1610 at Cupids (Cupere's Cove). Other settlements on the Avalon Peninsula were founded at Trepassey, Ferryland and Renews. Early settlers had to contend with the poor climatic conditions, lack of fertile soil for farming, and opposition by the merchants who tried to enforce the rule that settlers must reside six miles from any shore. The residential population remained smaller than the summer population until the latter 1700s. The dependency of Newfoundland residents on fishing was a key factor in the colony's slow growth, while other continental colonies offered more diverse enterprises. The Western Charter (1634) placed the authority of each harbour in the hands of the first ship's captain to arrive each spring. During the 1700s merchants set up permanent headquarters in Newfoundland and diversified their operations to include shipbuilding, trapping, seal hunting and trading. The records of merchants such as Slades, Lesters, and Newmans provide useful details of this period.

Conflict between European countries had an impact on Newfoundland; St. John's twice fell into French hands, in 1708 and 1757. From 1727 until 1817 the commander of the naval convoy that arrived each summer and departed each fall was made Governor and Commander-in-Chief. Surrogate judges or naval officers presided in larger outports. Certain French rights were established or clarified in the treaties of Utrecht (1713) and Versailles (1783). The colony was granted a year-round governor in 1817, and in 1832 the first election was held for a local House of Assembly.

In 1841, the British government suspended the constitution and responsible government was not granted until 1855, when Newfoundland became self-governing. In 1867, when the Dominion of Canada was established, Newfoundland chose not to participate in the union. In 1927 Labrador was awarded to Newfoundland by the Imperial Privy Council, and the province is therefore called "Newfoundland and Labrador". Following a short time as a dominion within the British Empire, Newfoundland lost self-government in 1934, when a Commission of three Newfoundlanders and three Englishmen was appointed to govern the colony. Finally in 1949, following a narrowly-contested plebiscite, Newfoundland became a province of Canada, with an elected and representative House of Assembly. England's oldest colony is Canada's newest province. The population (1986) was 568,349 people.

MAJOR REPOSITORIES

1. *Provincial Archives of Newfoundland & Labrador (P.A.N.L.)*

The records available at the Provincial Archives constitute the most important collection of government and private papers in the province. The P.A.N.L. was created in 1959 and falls under the Historic Resources Division, Dept. of Culture, Recreation and Youth. The site of the Archives is the Colonial Bldg., which was opened in 1850 as the home of the Provincial Parliament. The two large legislative chambers, each with 28-foot high ceilings, were more suited to that first purpose than to the present function of housing aging documents. Since the inception of the P.A.N.L. the collections have been considerably increased.

The family historian should begin his research here, because many appropriate records are found at the P.A.N.L. Copies of parish registers beginning in the late 1700s are more fully itemized below. These registers are mostly unindexed. Original parish registers are kept by the churches in the St. John's offices, which have suitable storage facilities, or in the parish offices.

The largest section of material at the Archives consists of government records, beginning with Colonial Office records, court records, voters lists, census returns, lists of inhabitants, customs records, and government departmental records, including those of the Registrar-General at the Registry of Vital Statistics from 1892 to 1915. Surrogate Court records date from 1787, Magistrates Courts from 1788, and Supreme Court records begin in 1795. Court records can provide information on estates, writs, and judgments, and may yield details about an elusive ancestor. Registry of Land Grants from 1815 may be studied at the Archives but copies are available only from the Registrar of Deeds or from Crown Lands Division.

The Private Papers collection contains parish registers (P8), many records of businesses and societies, and important collections donated by individuals. An Index to Private Papers is available. Business records of early Newfoundland merchants may offer clues about early settlers. Often the businesses were required to submit detailed reports to their home offices in England. Companies whose records, some on microfilm, others in the original, may be studied at the Archives, include Lester & Co., Trinity (who began business in the mid-1700s), O'Rourke's in Carbonear (1800s), Wiscombe's in Marystown, Slades (1780s), and Newman's. Apart from ledger books and accounts, these records include personnel items and indentures, and may offer the fortunate genealogist the origins of a family's first settler.

Other important material in the P.A.N.L. includes a large collection of films, audio tapes and photographic images. The Still and Moving Images Collection is available for viewing, either on videotape or in original photographic image. The Cartographic Collection has hundreds of historic maps, including both English and French maps of parts of early Newfoundland. Many of the detailed community maps show the original property owners. Copies of maps may be available when the condition of the original map permits reproduction. The Cartographic Archivist can advise if maps are available for the community being researched. The Crown Lands Division, Dept. of Forestry Services & Lands, will also make copies of community maps.

The P.A.N.L. employ a genealogist who will perform limited record searches. Lengthy research cannot be undertaken but the services of a professional researcher may be utilized. A list of researchers is available from the Archives. The Archives publication, *A Guide to the Government Records of Newfoundland*, compiled by Margaret Chang, is a useful reference tool, and other lists of archival holdings are available from the Archives.

Address:	Provincial Archives of Newfoundland & Labrador
	Colonial Bldg., Military Rd.
	St. John's, Newfoundland
	A1C 2C9
Telephone:	709-753-9390
Hours:	Monday to Friday 9:00 to 16:45;
	Wednesday & Thursday 18:30-21:45 as well.

2. *The Maritime History Archive* was established at Memorial University in 1971 to initiate and encourage research into all aspects of maritime history. The holdings of the Archive consist of materials relating to the history of sea-based activities, with emphasis on the north Atlantic. Collections relate to shipping, fisheries and commerce since 1600. A leaflet is available which describes records at the Archive of interest to genealogists.

Of prime interest is the Name File compiled by the late Dr. Keith Matthews. This collection of about 6,000 surnames developed from his research into the fisheries and settlement of Newfoundland from about 1640 to 1840. The data was obtained from mercantile, church, shipping and court records, as well as from newspapers and government and state papers.

This Archive houses Crew Agreements and Official Log Books, 1863-1938, pertaining to British vessels. These are indexed by the official number which was issued to each vessel. To research this material it is essential to know the name of the vessel on which a person served. Other holdings include certificates of vessel registry, colonial ports 1820-1920; Colonial Office Records; Admiralty Records; newspapers; Lloyd's Register of Shipping; mercantile, customs and census records; diaries and journals; port books for vessels entering and clearing western English ports; muster rolls; plantation books; apprenticeship indentures; and wills, inventories and parish records of Devon, Dorset and Newfoundland.

The Archive's researcher will undertake genealogical searches (except in the Devon and Dorset parish registers). A list of research fees is available upon request.

Address:	Maritime History Archive
	Henrietta Harvey Bldg.
	Memorial University
	St. John's, Newfoundland
	A1C 5S7

Contact:	Heather Wareham, archivist;
	Roberta Thomas, researcher

Telephone: 709-737-8428

Hours: Weekdays 9:00-17:00, closed for lunch hour

3. *Folklore and Language Archive* (MUNFLA) consists of student collections dealing with folklore, oral history and culture in Newfoundland and Labrador. Indexing of the records is chronological, from the year the record was made, and then by subject. Students contributed histories of their own communities. Family charts and student file questionnaires provide genealogical information. There are approximately 8,000 taped interviews of Newfoundlanders and these are indexed by subject. The Dr. Gerald Pocius Collection of photographs of headstones from the southern shore and the Brigus area is kept here.

E.R. Seary's work file (80-005) is housed at MUNFLA, and contains notes for his book, *Family Names of the Island of Newfoundland*. The files were compiled by students who studied sources such as year books, census returns, plantation books, parish records and newspapers to extract information on assigned surnames. The work files contain considerably more than the published book. There is a second part to the work file - a chronological index for some Newfoundland newspapers during the 1840s. Research may be done in person, by appointment, or by mail.

Address:	Folklore and Language Archive, Room E4038
	Education Bldg., Memorial University
	St. John's, Newfoundland
	A1C 5S7

Contact: Philip Hiscock, archivist

Telephone: 709-737-8401

Hours: By appointment

VITAL RECORDS

Civil registration began in 1891; earlier years must be searched in church registers of births, deaths and marriages. The Vital Statistics Division will search its post-1891 records for a search fee of $4.00 per three-year period. If they find the required records, a copy may be purchased for $10.00, with the $4.00 search fee being deducted from the price.

The P.A.N.L. has accumulated a large number of parish registers for the pre-1891 period. These are discussed in detail below, under the heading "Church Records".

Address: Vital Statistics Division
       Department of Health
       Confederation Bldg.
       St. John's, Newfoundland
       A1C 5T7

Telephone: 709-576-3308

CENSUS RECORDS

The first lists of residents in Newfoundland were those compiled by the French at Plaisance (Placentia). Both the P.A.N.L. and the National Archives of Canada (N.A.C.) possess copies of these. The early English lists were compiled as part of an attempt to end English residency on the island. The returns made prior to the island-wide 1836 census form part of the Colonial Office records and are for specific areas and purposes. The Centre for Newfoundland Studies, the Provincial Reference and Resource Library, and the Maritime History Archive, as well as the P.A.N.L. and the N.A.C., have many census records.

English census records for 1675-1884 include the following:

1675   Sir John Berry Census - list of planters from Cape de Razo to Cape Bonavista; names planters for thirty harbours.

1676   Captain Russell's Census - account of English inhabitants between Bonaventure and Petty Harbour; includes names in 18 settlements.

1677   Sir John Berry Census - Cape Race to Cape Bonavista; names each community, inhabitants, numbers of wives, children, servants, houses, boats, stages, animals, and pasture land.

1677	Sir William Poole's Census - Cape Bonavista to Trepassey; names inhabitants, numbers of wives, sons, etc., covering 28 settlements.
1675-77	A short list of planters at Renews in 1663 and a list of 19 planters in St. John's in 1669. The latter is by James Yonge.
1681	Captain James Story's Census - planters from Trepassey to Bonavista to Fair Island.
1682	Captain Daniel Jones' Census
1691 1693 1704	Census returns at the National Archives of Canada.
1702	Census of Trinity Bay lists five settlements.
1708	List of inhabitants in 28 settlements from Ferryland to Bonavista. This was the last comprehensive survey of the English Shore for over a century.
1713-14	William Taverner Survey of previously held French territory. (1671, 1673, 1698, 1706, 1711 French census material from Placentia is held at the N.A.C.).
1753	Census of Trinity, eleven settlements.
1794	Inhabitants in the harbour and district of St. John's including Bell Island, Petty Harbour, Portugal Cove and Torbay; gives names of the occupier and owner of the property, his occupation, the number of years he was in the country, religion, marital status, number of children and servants.
1796-97	Census of St. John's
1799-1800	Census of Ferryland, nominal list of masters and servants.
1800-01	Census of Trinity Bay, names occupiers and property owners in eighteen settlements.
1800-01	Register of families in Ferryland.
1804-06	List of Plantations in Conception Bay, which covers about 60 settlements from Bay de Verde to Holyrood. In 1820 additions were made for the area from Kelligrews to Portugal Cove. District magistrates in

other areas were also required to make similar returns which identi-
fied the claims of property holders to their land, but only Conception Bay's plantation book has survived. In the Colonial Office
records fragments of other returns are preserved.

1806   Register of Fishing Rooms for Bonavista Bay lists settlers between
              Bonavista and Greenspond.

1827-28   Populations of Newfoundland showing the districts of St. John's,
              Bay Bulls, Bonavista, Burin, Conception Bay, Ferryland, Fortune
              Bay, Fogo, Placentia, St. Mary's Trepassey and Trinity.

1836   Census of Fogo and Twillingate; surviving part of a larger census.

1838-39   List of inhabitants of the western shores of Newfoundland.

1849   List of settlers at Bay of Islands and Bonne Bay.

1858   List of settlers in distress at Bay St. George.

1884   Census of Burin.

In 1836, 1845, 1869, 1884, 1901, 1911, 1921, 1935 and 1945 official censuses of the
entire island were taken. Only the last two and parts of the 1911 and 1921 census
have survived in nominal form.

Information for this list of census returns has come from Dr. W. Gordon Handcock, Dept. of Geography at Memorial University, from David Davis, Archivist for
the Province of Newfoundland and Labrador, and from "Researching Your Family's History in Newfoundland and Labrador," published by the Newfoundland
and Labrador Genealogical Society.

Other Population Sources:

While census returns provide important information, they tend to be sporadic
and there are other means of filling gaps. Voters lists, year books and directories
are found either in manuscript form or copies at the P.A.N.L., Provincial Reference
& Resource Library, and at the Centre for Newfoundland Studies.

For example, the Provincial Reference & Resource Library has the following St.
John's and Newfoundland directories: 1864-65, 1870, 1871, 1885-86, 1890, 1894-97,
1898, 1904, 1908-09, 1913, 1915, 1924, 1928, 1932 and 1936. Year books are arranged

in order of community and region and offer the name and occupation of men over the voting age of 21. Women usually only appear if they were widows. City directories are listed by streets. One important directory has been indexed, namely, *Lovell's Province of Newfoundland Directory for 1871, containing Names of Professional and Business Men, and other Inhabitants in the Cities, Towns, and Villages throughout the Province.* Interesting statistics are included in a historical sketch. Copies of the index may be viewed at all major repositories. Other directories are similar in content.

All pre-confederation records (1949) are open to public viewing, giving Newfoundlanders access to twentieth-century government records not available elsewhere. Enumerators books for 1911, 1921, 1935 and 1945 may be consulted at the P.A.N.L., although a few books are missing. Voters lists are filed under the reference number GN43. The manuscript voters lists (GN43/7) are:

Bay Roberts - 1855, 1858, 1878, 1885
Bishops Cove - 1845, 1848, 1849, 1855, 1865, 1868, 1869, 1878, 1882, 1889
Bryants Cove - 1847, 1858, 1865, 1868, 1874, 1885, 1889
Carbonear - 1847, 1855
Conception Bay - 1835, 1844, 1847, 1849
Ferryland - 1840-41, 1859
Harbour Grace - 1832, 1843, 1855, 1858, 1861, 1865, 1868, 1874, 1878, 1885, 1889,
    1893, 1919
Harbour Main - 1874, 1884 (9?), 1919
Island Cove - 1847, 1848, 1855, 1858, 1865, 1868, 1869, 1874, 1878, 1885, 1889
Mosquito - 1847
Port de Grave-Brigus - 1889
Spaniards Bay 1855, 1858, 1865, 1868, 1873, 1882, 1885, 1889
Trinity District 1889, 1893
Western Bay - 1847, 1848, 1849.

LAND RECORDS

There are two main sources of information for land ownership: Crown Lands Administration and the Registry of Deeds.

Crown Lands Administration hold records for the original owners of land. Grants and leases were issued in the early 1800s. All grants are arranged in a Geographical Index, starting in St. John's and then divided by bays or coasts. Listing is chronological but not all grants have survived as several volumes were destroyed by fire. Copies of grants may be purchased and some indexes show a plan number for the cadastral map on which the grant is plotted. These maps show the lands granted or leased by the Crown and will show names of the property owners and various features that existed at the time of the survey. Records covering residential, agriculture, mining and timber leases are also at the Crown Lands Administration.

Crown Lands Administration,
Government of Newfoundland & Labrador,
Department of Forestry Services and Lands,
Lands Branch, Howley Building, Higgins Line,
St. John's Newfoundland
A1C 5T7
709-576-3085 (Hours 9-5 weekdays)

The Registry of Deeds is the official administrative centre for registered land conveyances. The land deeds on file date from about 1825 and are filed annually. There is an alphabetical index for each year both of the buyers' and seller's surnames. A miscellaneous collection of wills dating from 1744 should not be overlooked. These records are open to the public and a $1 search fee applies for those able to visit in person. No inquiries will be accepted by mail but a list of companies which provide searching services is available upon request.

Government of Newfoundland and Labrador,
Registry of Deeds, Companies and Securities,
P.O. Box 4750,
Confederation Building,
St. John's, Newfoundland
A1C 5T7
709-576-3317 (hours 9-5 weekdays)

PROBATE RECORDS

The main repository for probate records is the Registrar's Office, Supreme Court of Newfoundland, Duckworth St., St. John's, Nfld., A1C 5M3. Apart from wills there are inventories of property, letters of administration, letters of probate, trusteeships, guardianships, bonds, and depositions. Wills up to 1899 are on microfilm at the P.A.N.L. and may be consulted there in person only. An index of wills up to 1945 may also be viewed in person at the P.A.N.L. Inquiries by mail must be addressed to the Registrar, Supreme Court, the only authority able to issue copies. The telephone number is 709-726-4482.

The Supreme Court has wills on file from about 1830 until the present. They are filed chronologically, with alphabetical indexes for each year. For $1. a search will be made for a will, which may then be copied for 30¢ per page. When requesting a search it is helpful to give as much information as possible in order to assist the Registrar in identifying the pertinent record. Few people made wills in Newfoundland in the 1800s but if your ancestor did, then you will find useful information and perhaps a signature if he could write. Consider also applying for wills belonging to lateral relatives as well as direct ancestors. It is possible, for example, for your great grandfather to receive a mention in his uncle's will. Even if he does not, the will could at least expand your knowledge of the family circle.

CHURCH RECORDS

Considering that civil registration was not required in Newfoundland until 1891, church records assume great importance. Many of the parish registers have been copied by the P.A.N.L. Some are photocopies of the original records; others are handwritten copies made during a province-wide project to bring as many copies of records as possible to the P.A.N.L. However, these handmade copies do contain errors made during transcription. The P.A.N.L. will consult the parish registers in their files but will not issue photocopies. The original registers remain with the church authorities, either at the parish or at the church offices in St. John's. Because churches tended to be constructed of wood, they were prone to fire and thus many records have been lost.

The clergy had charge of large parishes and maintained their registers in circuit books covering several communities. As there are generally no indexes in parish registers, careful researching is needed, watching for the occasional change of community name. Some parish registers have survived even if the church burned, since the books were located elsewhere. A letter to the pastor of the community may locate parish records and even present-day relatives.

The Church of England was the official church in Newfoundland from 1583, when Humphrey Gilbert formally took posession of the island. The first clergymen to reside in Newfoundland came under the sponsorship of the Society for the Propagation of the Gospel in Foreign Parts (S.P.G.). The Society was formed in England in 1701 for the purpose of sending Anglican missionaries to parts of the British Empire which could not support their own clergy. During the 1700s, S.P.G. clergymen were stationed at St. John's Bay Bulls, Bonavista, Ferryland, Harbour Grace, Placentia and Trinity Bay. These missionaries were required to send to their home office (Lambeth Palace) regular reports containing lists of subscribers, reports on the conditions of life and other salient comments. The reports are available on microfilm at the P.A.N.L., and at Queen Elizabeth II Library, Microform Room. The microfilm is entitled "The Fulham Papers at Lambeth Palace Library" which comprises 42 volumes on twenty reels (Microfilm

3636). World Microfilm Productions, London, published this set; reels 1, 11 and 19 refer to Newfoundland. The film is of the original records and requires great concentration to decipher, but the result may be worthwhile as other records for the 1700s are few. The S.P.G. supported Anglican ministers in Newfoundland until 1922.

Until the 1760s the Church of England was the only form of religion regularly practiced in Newfoundland. In 1765 Rev. Laurence Coughlan introduced Methodism (Wesleyism) at Harbour Grace, and Roman Catholicism was introduced in the 1780s. The Church of England remained the official church. From 1787 until 1825 Newfoundland formed part of the See of Nova Scotia, and from 1839 until 1919 the See of Newfoundland included both Labrador and Bermuda. In 1775 the first Congregationalist minister arrived in St. John's and managed to establish missions in other parts of the island by the 1780s. The Congregational Church merged with the Presbyterian Church in 1938. The latter had been established in St. John's in 1842 by the growing number of Scottish immigrants. From 1850 to 1878 two Presbyterian churches, the Kirk and the Free Church of St. Andrew's, operated separately in St. John's. Following the burning of both churches in 1878, they united to build one new church.

The majority of the population were either Anglicans or Roman Catholics. In 1886 the Salvation Army was established in St. John's and has grown to a large following throughout the island. In 1942 Methodists joined with some Congregationalist and Presbyterian churches to adhere to the United Church of Canada.

Researching Parish Registers:

The earliest Anglican registers start around 1790 but most are more recent. Some Roman Catholic registers start around 1810 but the marriage register for St. John's Basilica begins in 1793. Presbyterian registers begin in 1842 and those of the Salvation Army date from 1886. The genealogist at the P.A.N.L. will make brief searches in the parish registers. Each denomination has a central office which may house archival material. Written inquiries for information from original parish registers may be addressed to one of the following, as appropriate:

Diocesan Synod of Eastern Newfoundland
Anglican Church of Canada
c/o Archdeacon Oake
19 King's Bridge Road
St. John's, Newfoundland
A1C 3K4

Roman Catholic Archives
Archdiocese of St. John's
c/o Sister Clothilde Meaney, Assistant Archivist
Box 1363
St. John's, Newfoundland
A1C 5N5

United Church Archives
Mr. F. Burnham Gill, Archivist
320 Elizabeth Avenue
St. John's, Newfoundland
A1B 1T9

Divisional Headquarters
Salvation Army
21 Adams Avenue
St. John's, Newfoundland
A1C 4Z1

Presbytery of Newfoundland
17 Church Rd.
Grand Falls, Newfoundland
A2A 1Z4

Queen's College Archives
(Anglican)
Dr. Hans Rollman
Memorial University
St. John's, Newfoundland
A1C 5S7

The P.A.N.L. possesses a collection of original or copied church registers for the principal denominations. (**A** - Anglican, **C** - Catholic, **P** - Presbyterian, **U** - United). In 1987 these holdings comprised the following:

PLACE		*BAPTISMS*	*MARRIAGES*	*BURIALS*
Argentia	C	1835-1897	1835-1896	
Baie Verte/White Bay S.	U		1906-1933	1906-1933
Bareneed	A	1839-1863	1829-1863	
Bay Bulls	C	1830-1933	1876-1956	1911-1965
Bay Bulls Arm	U	1917-1967	1917-1968	
Bay de Verde	A	1841-1874	1841-1893	1874-1900
Bay Roberts	A	1837-1907	1835-1892	1843-1907

Bay of Islands	A	1864-1958	1870-1978	1870-1980
Bay St. George	A	1880-1961	1880-1974	1881-1983
	U	1883-1969	1875-1969	1875-1915
Black Head	U	1842-1970	1842-1970	1883-1947
Bonavista	A	1786-1834	1786-1834	1786-1973
	U	1817-1884	1836-1916	1827-1947
Bonavista-Trinity	C	1842-1944	1844-1915	1894-1944
Bonne Bay	A	1871-1879	1871-1879	1871-1879
	U	1874-1936	1875-1952	
Botwood	U	1889-1963	1890-1958	1890-1948
Brigus	A		1830	
	U	1822-1982	1823-1984	1824-1981
Brigus Parish	C			1882-1913
Britannia Cove	U	1883-1957	1883-1957	1884-1958
Burgeo	U	1880-1959	1884-1959	1882-1954
Burin	C	1833-1955	1833-1904	
	U	1816-1983	1816-1972	1816-1985
Burnt Is. (Exploits)	U	1860-1893		
Cambellton/Stoneville	U	1906-1981	1906-1981	1906-1981
Carbonear	A	1834-1913	1859-1908	1849-1953
	C	1849-1901	1850-1883	
	U	1817-1908	1794-1967	1820-1888
Carmanville	U		1917-1985	1906-1946
Catalina	A	1834-1879	1833-1879	1829-1942
Change Islands	U	1917-1933		1947-1967
Channel	A		1929-1940	
Clarenville	U		1921-1939	
Conception Hbr.	C	1884-1945	1884-1930	
Conche	C	1873-1981		1902-1981
Cupids	A			1860-1895
	U	1842-1922	1837-1930	
Englee	U	1882-1947	1883-1981	1883-1968
Exploits	U	1908-1944	1908-1954	1908-1958
Ferryland	C	1870-1910	1870-1910	
Flowers Cove	U	1874-1964	1874-1942	1874-1964
Fogo Island/Change Is.	A	1841-1879	1841-1972	1879-1972
		1901-1917		
		1943-1972		
Fogo Island	U	1863-1972	1890-1972	1890-1972
Freshwater Victoria	U	1887-1946	1883-1948	1883-1962
Green Bay Circuit	U	1841-1853	1842-1878	
Greenspond	U	1862-1876	1862-1886	1862-1924
Harbour Buffett	A	1890-1958	1914-1955	1913-1985
Harbour Grace	A	1775-1916	1776-1917	1775-1917
	C	1806-1945	1812-1892	
	U	1820-1899		

Harbour Main	C	1857-1899	1857-1905	
Heart's Content	A	1879-1903	1879-1960	1886-1973
	U	1911-1986	1917-1986	1915-1986
Holyrood	C	1880-1905	1883-1909	
Horwood	U	1917-1933		
King's Cove, Trinity	C	1815-1909	1815-1909	
King's Point	U	1911-1933	1911-1936	1911-1933
Lamaline	A	1849-1859		
Long Island/Little Bay Is.	U	1865-1964	1867-1967	1874-1964
Lower Island Cove	U	1816-1891	1850-1935	1838-1894
Marystown	C	1895-1922		
Milton	U		1961-1981	
Musgravetown	U		1938-1959	
Northern Bay	C	1838-1871	1838-1914	
Old Perlican	U	1853-1901	1816-1941	1882-1910
Pilley's Is.	U	1909-1932	1909-1975	1909-1978
Placentia	C	1846-1921	1822-1921	1896-1934
Port de Grave	A	1827-1842	1828-1839	1828-1869
Port de Grave/ Clarke's Beach	U	1889-1938	1837-1959	1913-1951
Portugal Cove	C	1844-1893	1886-1892	
Pouch Cove	A	1841-1946	1841-1970	1841-1976
	U	1878-1917	1879-1914	1903-1916
Random (Trinity Bay)	A	1880-1985	1880-1984	1880-1980
	U	1890-1956	1892-1969	
Renews	C	1857-1919	1838-1920	
St. Anthony	U	1893-1890	1830-1890	
St. Georges	A	1841-1852	1841-1896	1841-1871
St. John's	A	1810-1870	1830-1879	1865-1869
St. John's St. Andrew's (The Kirk)	P	1842-1969	1842-1969	1879-1914
St. John's Basilica	C	1802-1886	1793-1890	
St. John's Cathedral- West Coast, Northern Peninsula and Labrador	A	1790-1906	1752-1879	1752-1906
St. Mary's	C	1843-1898	1844-1898	1891-1898
Shoal Harbour, Trinity Bay	U	1918-1942	1939-1975	1892-1962
Tilting	C	1842-1904	1842-1904	
Topsail	A	1833-1905	1861-1935	1833-1869
	U	1886-1982	1886-1982	
Trepassey	C	1843-1909	1861-1868	1856-1915
Trinity	A	1753-1826		
Twillingate	A	1816-1823		
	U	1853-1878	1853-1876	1852-1882
Victoria	U	1908-1952	1921-1975	1910-1938

Wesley Circuit	U	1905-1919	1905-1923	1905-1938
Western Bay	U	1817-1970	1899-1963	1908-1970
Whitbourne	C	1891-1921	1891-1921	1892-1921
	U	1892-1917	1893-1917	1893-1917
Witless Bay	C	1830-1949	1830-1880	1901-1908

Labrador:

Hopedale Moravian		1850-1975		
Killinek Moravian		1850-1925		
Nain (Hebron)	U	1940-1942	1940	
North West River	U	1884-1950	1885-1945	1884-1951
Red Bay	U	1877-1973	1878-1973	1878-1972
Sandwich Bay	U			1906-1913

Births 1886-1976 and marriages 1921-1945, of all districts of the Salvation Army form P8/A/12 at the P.A.N.L. The Salvation Army was active, for example, in Bonavista, Burgeo-La Poile, Burin, Fogo, Fortune-Hermitage, Grand Falls, Green Bay, Harbour Grace, Harbour Main, Humber, Placentia, Port de Grave, St. Barbe, Trinity and Twillingate.

In addition to the holdings of the P.A.N.L., the Maritime History Archive possesses copies of other registers for Newfoundland communities (e.g., the Anglican Church at Trinity, 1753-1840).

CEMETERY RECORDS

Until recently little effort was made to preserve information on headstones. Hundreds of outports were abandoned as part of a government resettlement plan in the 1960s. Not only have these communities fallen into disrepair, but the valuable information in the churchyards has suffered from erosion and neglect. Some historical and heritage societies have recorded the inscriptions on the headstones while other communities buried their headstones and planted a lawn over them.

In 1985 the Newfoundland and Labrador Genealogical Society began an island-wide awareness program. Rural development associations and historical societies in about sixty communities were contacted and asked to co-operate in recording cemetery inscriptions. The result of this communication has been that many communities have already recorded their inscriptions and donated copies of the work to the P.A.N.L. and to the church offices. Other communities have expressed an interest in ensuring that this work be done in the future. The Newfoundland and Labrador Genealogical Society has a policy of publishing any projects undertaken by members of the Society or donated to it. Five publications by the Society have appeared: Topsail Anglican Cemetery Inscriptions, Cupids United Church Inscriptions, Cemetery Inscriptions from Labrador, Cemetery Inscriptions from the Northern Peninsula, and Cemetery Inscriptions from the Town of Fortune.

The importance of the headstone inscriptions for genealogical research in Newfoundland cannot be over-emphasized. Many of our ancestors arrived here in the 1700 and 1800s, during a time when the government did not require the recording of vital statistics. The most promising method of locating the place of origin of one's ancestor is from the inscription on a headstone, many of which survive from that time. The first headstones actually made in Newfoundland date from about 1830; previously the stones had been imported from Ireland, England or New England. People who could not afford the luxury of an imported headstone would have had wooden markers, but these have not survived for various reasons. The author, however, has seen wooden head markers which have survived and remained legible for eighty years.

Death records are of less value than the inscriptions on headstones. The death record will not give the place of birth or the names of wife and children. While the parish registers vary according to the preference of individual clergymen, all tend to be restricted in the amount of information they give. Some cemetery work is discussed later, under the heading "Special Projects".

IMMIGRATION

As early as the 1600s fishermen from England, France, Portugal and Spain sailed each summer to the fertile fishing banks off Newfoundland. No doubt some of these people found reasons to over-winter on the island, as had been the custom of the Basque whalers in the Strait of Belle Isle in the previous century. Long before the major European powers were struggling for colonies and empires in the Orient, there was a quiet colonization of the island of Newfoundland. Although the official colonies of the early 1600s (beginning with the John Guy settlement at Cupids, 1610) were unsuccessful, continuous English settlement soon took root. Newfoundland never held the allure of the settlements in New England or Virginia, which offered a diversity unattainable on "the Rock". Settlers in Newfoundland remained dependent on the fishing trade and no alternatives were available to sustain life. The climate and soil conditions of the island were unsuited to more than minimal farming, while severe winter conditions were a further deterrent to would-be settlers. Newfoundland became a gateway through which thousands of settlers passed on their way to continental North America. To this day, the people of Newfoundland continue to populate the towns and cities of Canada and the United States.

Until the early 1700s the population of the island is estimated to have been small: about 5,000 in 1690 reduced to about 2,300 in 1720. The population fluctuations resulted from failures of the fishery, wars in Europe, or the departure of settlers either back home or on to New England. The early settlers in Newfoundland came from Devon, Dorset, Hampshire, and Somerset ("the west country"), and from the Channel Islands. From the early 1700s the population began to increase steadily and many of the newcomers were from southern Ireland, in particular from the counties Kilkenny, Tipperary, Waterford and Wexford.

French settlement was centered at Plaisance (Placentia) until 1713, when the Treaty of Utrecht established the "French Shore". Because many early French settlers were illegal residents on the west coast, they left few records. They were ministered to by Irish priests who spoke no French. Some Acadians came from across the Gulf of St. Lawrence and Cape Breton. Others came directly from France, generally from Brittany and Normandy. There are about one hundred family names of French origin currently in use in Newfoundland, and main centres of French settlement are located in the Port-au-Port Peninsula, St. Georges and the Codroy Valley. The Centre d'Etudes Franco-Terreneuviennes at Memorial University, under director Dr. Gerald Thomas, has an archive which contains orally recorded data, some of which is transcribed. Written inquiries may be addressed to Dr. Thomas, who has published articles on French and Acadian family names in the journal *Onomastica Canadiana*, Vol. 62, pp. 23-34 (Dec. 1982) and Vol. 68, pp.21-33 (June 1986). The French who settled St. Pierre and Miquelon islands off the south coast of Newfoundland have had close ties with the people of Newfoundland. Some settlers may have served with the French navy. There are two addresses of use when writing to France to seek information on French ancestors:

La Conservateur-en-Chef, Chargé de la section Outre'Mer
Ministére de la Culture et de la Communication
Direction des Archives de France
27 rue Oudinot, F74007
Paris, France

Service Historique de la Marine
Pavillon de la Reine, Château de Vincennes
F94300 Vincennes, France
(these navy records begin in the 1600s)

The population of the island grew during the 1700s to about 20,000 residents by the 1790s. The slow growth was caused by several factors: official discouragement of year-round settlement, numerous wars, and the capacity of seasonal fishery to satisfy merchants. The nineteenth century was a period of much more rapid growth (nearly 200,000 by 1884) and a wider diversity of occupations, including lumbering and the mining of copper and iron ore. The population continued to be concentrated in small harbours and bays around the coast and settlers moved northward to find fishing rooms in less crowded harbours where, in addition to fishing, sealing on the drift ice each spring became popular.

The people of Newfoundland have always been mobile, moving around the island by boat, emigrating east or west. When the railway opened at the turn of the century more mobility was possible and many people began to leave the small harbours and settle in the larger towns where work opportunities could be found. This trend has continued to the present, and many outports were abandoned with government assistance in the 1960s.

NEWSPAPERS

Over a hundred newspapers have been published in Newfoundland at various times. Many towns had a weekly or semi-weekly newspaper, but few original newspapers have been preserved. The repository for surviving issues of Newfoundland newspapers is the Provincial Reference & Resource Library, Arts and Culture Centre, Allandale Rd., St. John's, Newfoundland. A1B 3A3. By 1988 other libraries and archives will have given their collections of original newspapers to the Library, keeping those which have been microfilmed. Although relatively few originals have survived, the remaining issues contain a wealth of information. Newspapers from small communities would often list all vessels arriving and departing along the coastline, mentioning passengers by name. These passengers might be mentioned in connection with a family, giving new clues to broaden the genealogy. Events which affected the region were reported. Before the days of roads and rail, communication links were by sea and important news would travel in the same manner.

At the P.A.N.L. copies of vital statistics are available from the following newspapers: *Harbour Grace Weekly Journal*, 1828-1838; *Harbour Grace Standard*, 1862-1872, 1875-1890, 1893, 1894; *The Star*, 1840-1843, 1872-1875; *Twillingate Sun*, 1945-1947, 1951-1952; and *The Weekly Herald*, 1849-1850.

Two other sources of extracts from Newfoundland newspapers are available. Gertrude Crosbie has published several books of vital records from newspapers, most recently *Births, Deaths and Marriages in Newfoundland Newspapers 1825-1850*, published in September 1986 by the Maritime History Archive. Data came from the following: *Carbonear Sentinel and Conception Bay Advertiser, Courier, Gazette, Weekly Herald of Harbour Grace, Ledger, Indicator, Mercury, Newfoundlander, Newfoundland Mercantile Journal, Post, Patriot, Star, Times, Vindicator*. Mrs. Crosbie's other work continues the extracts to 1867. Copies may be purchased from the Maritime History Archive.

Mrs. Mildred Howard, R.R. #2, Sydney, Nova Scotia B1P 6G4, has published four books of vital statistics from Newfoundland newspapers. Her first three publications are out of print but are available at the P.A.N.L. Publication number four, *Vital Statistics and Items from the Royal Gazette and Newfoundland Advertiser from 1810 to 1845*, is available from Mrs. Howard. Apart from the records of births, deaths and marriages, Mrs. Howard's publications include public notices, court records, petitions, passenger lists and dramatic events. She includes an alphabetical index of vessels as well as an index of surnames.

Those newspapers which have been microfilmed may be obtained through the inter-library loan service. A short list of some major newspapers is as follows:

1) *Newfoundlander*, published 1806-1884. Each issue contained local and foreign and shipping news. It supported Catholic opinion and Liberal politics. Published in St. John's.

2) *Royal Gazette and Newfoundland and General Advertiser*, first published in St. John's in 1807; since 1926 called the *Newfoundland Gazette*. It was a weekly and published, in addition to usual newspaper items, official notices, budgets, important speeches, and census reports.

3) *Public Ledger and Newfoundland General Advertiser*, published 1820-1882; after 1859 called the *Daily Ledger*. It supported Protestant opinion and Conservative politics.

4) *The Harbour Grace and Carbonear Weekly Journal and General Advertiser for Conception Bay*, published weekly in Harbour Grace from 1828, covered local and a small amount of foreign news.

5) *The Times and General Commercial Gazette*, published in St. John's bi-weekly 1832-1894. A partial index for some of the early years, compiled as part of the project of E.R. Seary's *Family Names of the Island of Newfoundland*, may be consulted at the Folklore and Language Archive, Memorial University, St. John's, Newfoundland. A1C 5S7.

6) *The Newfoundland Patriot*, published weekly in St. John's 1834-1878, was a political rival of the *Public Ledger*.

7) *The Evening Telegram,* published daily from 1879, remains St. John's major daily newspaper.

8) *The Western Star,* published semi-weekly from 1900, contains news and items from the Bay of Islands and Western Newfoundland.

9) *St. John's Daily News,* published 1860-1984.

Newspapers were published on a regular basis in Bay Roberts, Bay of Islands, Bell Island, Carbonear, Harbour Grace, Trinity, and Twillingate, as well as St. John's. A complete listing for Newfoundland newspapers has been published by Memorial University of Newfoundland in Suzanne Ellison's *Historical Directory of Newfoundland and Labrador Newspapers 1807-1987.*

SPECIAL PROJECTS

In the last five years there has been a dramatic increase in public interest in the history of Newfoundland and Labrador. The Newfoundland Historical Society holds well-attended meetings, the Humanities Association and the Museum Association of Newfoundland and Labrador hold workshops, and several new societies have formed. The Association of Newfoundland and Labrador Archivists, the Wessex Society of Newfoundland, and the Newfoundland and Labrador Genealogical Society are testimony to the surge of interest in our heritage and in conserving the records which allow us to explore the past. Associations around the Province are active in preserving historic records, and cemeteries are being restored and the inscriptions on headstones recorded. In particular the Carbonear Heritage Society made use of a Summer Work Grant to hire students in 1983 to record the inscriptions of the United Church in Carbonear, the Church of England in Carbonear, St. Patrick's Church in Carbonear, and the United Church at Freshwater. About 1500 headstone inscriptions were transcribed and copies of the work were donated to the churches and to the Provincial Archives.

During the last several summers the Bonavista Historical Society has been using similar grants to compile indexes of their parish registers. The project is expected to last two to three more summers and the completed index will be presented to the Provincial Archives.

Happy news comes from Them Days Archives in Happy Valley. A National Archives of Canada Grant has enabled Them Days to index their considerable collections which relate to Labrador. Their address is Box 939, Station B, Happy Valley - Goose Bay, Labrador, A0P 1E0. The telephone number is 709-896-8531.

The mandate of the Newfoundland and Labrador Genealogical Society is to make genealogical material, wherever located, available to those who seek it. In 1985 a Cemetery Cataloguing Committee was formed and immediately it began a province-wide awareness project. All Rural Development associations and historical societies (about 60) were contacted and the Genealogical Society is compiling a list of cemeteries which have already been transcribed. A special project began in 1985 with the permission of the Roman Catholic Archdiocese of St. John's. Belvedere Cemetery, St. John's has about 4,000 headstones, and, because the chapel burned in the 1920s, all early death records were lost. The Genealogical Society has been working in Belvedere Cemetery recording the inscriptions. Many inscriptions refer to people born in Ireland or England and may therefore offer the only reference to the birthplaces of these settlers. In addition to the Belvedere project members and friends of the Society are copying cemetery inscriptions all over the province, a work that insures that the amount of material available for genealogists is increasing. To request information or to offer assistance write to the Chairman, Cemetery Cataloguing Committee, Newfoundland and Labrador Genealogical Society, Colonial Bldg., Military Rd., St. John's, Newfoundland, A1C 2C9.

LIBRARIES & SOCIETIES

1) *Centre for Newfoundland Studies, Queen Elizabeth II Library* was established in 1965 as a special collection for the preservation and acquisition of material on Newfoundland and Labrador. It has since become the largest repository of published material on Newfoundland and the collection includes rare books, personal papers, manuscripts, diaries, government documents, periodicals, maps, theses, census returns, and the records of many societies and businesses. The Centre uses the closed stack method and identification is required before consultation of material. All items remain in the Centre and must be used in the reading room. The card catalogue contains author, title, and subject entries.

Many census returns are found here, as are records on microfilm such as reports from the Newfoundland School Society, the Society for the Education of the Poor (from 1823 - microfilm 619), and Newfoundland Church Society Reports (1847-1874 - microfilm 604).

The Centre has published *A Guide to the Archival Holdings of the Centre for Newfoundland Studies, Memorial University Library*, compiled in 1983 by Nancy Grenville.

Address: Centre for Newfoundland Studies
                  Queen Elizabeth II Library
                  Memorial University
                  St. John's, Newfoundland
                  A1B 3Y1

Contact: Anne Hart, head; Nancy Grenville, archivist

Hours: Monday to Friday 8:30-17:00; extended hours during
                  term:
                  Monday-Thursday 8:30-23:00, Friday 8:30-22:00,
                  Saturday 10:00-18:00, Sunday 13:30-22:00

Telephone: 709-737-7475

2) *Provincial Reference and Resource Library, (PRRL)* is the main repository for surviving Newfoundland newspapers. Other centres will have some microfilmed newspapers. Copies of some of the early census material are here. Most St. John's and Newfoundland directories are here, beginning with 1864-65. Newfoundland Year Books (almanacs) form part of the collection, as do voters lists and a comprehensive collection of published works.

The general reference section of the library contains many genealogical reference works. A list of these is available upon request and will provide a ready reference of leading genealogical books. Material is available through the Inter-Library Loan Service and microfilms of census returns and parish registers may be borrowed from the Public Archives of Canada.

The librarians in the Newfoundland Section are well qualified to assist the family historian. They receive many inquiries through the mail and many people visit the Library to undertake research.

Address: Provincial Reference and Resource Library
                  Newfoundland Section
                  Arts and Culture Centre
                  Allandale Road
                  St. John's, Newfoundland
                  A1B 3A3

Hours: Monday-Thursday 10:00 - 21:30
                  Friday, Saturday 10:00-17:00, closed Sunday

Mid-June to mid-September summer hours are in
effect: Monday-Thursday 10:00-20:30,
Friday 10:00-17:30, closed Saturday and Sunday

Telephone: 709-737-3954

3) *Corner Brook City Library* is the resource branch of the Western Regional Library.
Its collection includes general genealogical works and some volumes which are
specifically concerned with Newfoundland, such as Jane Hutching's *Early settlers
on the South-Western Shore of Newfoundland's Northern Peninsula*, Cavell Tyrell's *Butt
Family of the West Coast of Newfoundland*, and Agnes O'Dea's *Bibliography of Newfoundland*.

Copies of census returns for 1891 (vols. 1-3), 1901 (vols. 1-4) and 1921 (vols. 1-5),
and city directories for Corner Brook since 1967 are available. The library has
some recent St. John's city directories and copies of the 1870 Newfoundland directory and the 1877 Business Directory for Newfoundland.

The Corner Brook newspaper, *The Western Star*, is on microfilm from 1907 to
the present. Originals are kept only until the microfilm is received. Issues of the
newspaper are sporadic until 1951 and until 1967 there are missing numbers. One
reel of microfilm contains all surviving issues from April 1907 to December 1916,
compared to today's issues which require six reels per year.

Church and parish registers on microfilm cover a variety of years and may include births, baptisms, marriages or burials. The key places with microfilmed
records in this Library are:

Badger's Quay (Anglican)
Battle Harbour (Anglican)

Bay of Islands (Anglican)
Bay of St. George (Anglican)
Bonavista (Anglican & Methodist)

Burgeo (Anglican)
Burin & Grand Bank (Methodist)

Change Islands (Anglican)
Channel (Anglican & United)

Fogo Island (Anglican)
Gloverstown (Anglican &
  Methodist)

Heart's Delight (Anglican)
Musgravetown (Anglican
  & Methodist)

Nippers Harbour
  (Methodist)
Rose Blanche (Anglican)
Trinity (Anglican)
Twillingate (Methodist)

The library will reply to genealogical enquiries by mail for those people with west coast origins.

Address: Corner Brook City Library
                Sir Richard Squires Bldg.
                Corner Brooks, Newfoundland
                A2H 6J8

Hours: Monday-Friday 10:00-21:00, year round
                Saturday 10:00-17:30, September to June
                Sunday 14:00-17:00, November to March

Telephone: 709-637-2220.

4) *Kindale Public Library* contains the regional archive of the Bay of St. George/Port-au-Port Heritage Association.

Address: Kindale Public Library
                16 Glendale St.
                Stephenville, Newfoundland
                A2N 2K3

Telephone: 709-643-4262

5) *Newfoundland Historical Society* was established in 1881. Its aims include the preservation of all printed books, manuscripts and records having reference to Newfoundland. In spite of some inactive periods, the Society has continued and has an office. Community histories, newspapers clippings and personal correspondence are of special interest to genealogists. The Society produces a newsletter and contributes regularly to the *Newfoundland Quarterly* through a column entitled "Aspects". Meetings are held regularly, except during the summer.

Address: Newfoundland Historical Society
                Room 15, Colonial Bldg.
                Military Road
                St. John's, Newfoundland
                A1C 2C7

Hours: Monday-Friday 9:00-12:00

6) *Newfoundland and Labrador Genealogical Society, Inc.*, was founded in 1984 to encourage and help genealogists with a particular interest in their Newfoundland

ancestry. The Society was incorporated in 1987. Regular meetings and newsletters provide members with information, as do the facilities available at the Society's office. The Society recently published a brochure of genealogical sources in the province and has published several books of cemetery inscriptions. A growing library of genealogies and published materials is housed in the office. In 1985 the Society spearheaded a province-wide appeal to awaken interest in recording headstone information. Membership is world-wide, with a large number of members in mainland North America that reflects the pattern of emigration from Newfoundland. Members publish their research interests in the newsletters and can locate those with similar interests. The office may be visited by appointment only.

> Address: Newfoundland and Labrador Genealogical Society
>   Colonial Bldg., Military Rd.
>   St. John's, Newfoundland
>   A1C 2C9
>   (Office: Room 240, Harvey Rd. Bldg.)

Staff at the P.A.N.L. may be contacted concerning meetings.

7) *Wessex Society of Newfoundland* was founded in 1984 with the Hon. A. Brian Peckford, Premier of Newfoundland and Labrador, as its patron. The purpose of the Society is to stimulate interest in, and knowledge of, Newfoundland origins in the west country of England. The word Wessex harkens back to the early kingdoms of England, and refers to present-day Devon, Dorset, parts of Hampshire, Somerset, Cornwall and Wiltshire, areas of heavy migration to early Newfoundland. The Society holds meetings, usually in the Education Bldg., Room 5004, Memorial University.

> Address: Wessex Society of Newfoundland
>   Dept. of Geography
>   Memorial University
>   St. John's, Newfoundland
>   A1C 5S7

> Contact: Dr. W. Gordon Handcock, Secretary-Treasurer

PERIODICALS

The following list includes some publications which are totally genealogical in their content, such as *The Newfoundland Ancestor* and *Halfyard Heritage*. The other periodicals contain articles which are interesting and helpful for those researching family history in Newfoundland. Periodicals of general interest to all Atlantic Canada are included for their Newfoundland content.

1) *Acadiensis*, published twice a year by the Department of History, University of New Brunswick, Campus House, Fredericton, New Brunswick E3B 5A3. *Acadiensis* contains scholarly historical articles on Atlantic Canada. It includes original research articles, documents, reviews and a running bibliography of regional history. It has been published since 1971 and a cumulative index from 1971 - 1983 is available.

2) *Atlantic Guardian* (now *Atlantic Advocate*) was last published in Nova Scotia in 1957. Its platform was "To make Newfoundland better known at home and abroad; To promote trade and travel in the island; To encourage development of the Island's natural resources; To foster good relations between Newfoundland and her neighbors." Each monthly issue contained general articles of topical interest, poetry, history and biographies. Copies should be available through the public library system. *The Atlantic Advocate*, Box 3370, 12 Prospect St. W., Fredericton, N.B., E3B 5A2, is published monthly and contains articles of historical and geographical interest about Atlantic Canada.

3) *Atlantic Insight* is published monthly by Insight Publishing Ltd., 1656 Barrington St., Halifax, N.S. B3J 2A2. Articles cover many topics of life in Atlantic Canada and often focus on the history and culture of a town or region.

4) *Decks Awash* is published by Memorial University Extension Service, Memorial University, St. John's, Newfoundland, A1C 5S7. *Decks Awash* contains many community histories which form an essential part of a genealogist's research. For example, Volume 15, Number 6 (November-December 1986) includes a 60 page article on the communities of the Southwest Arm, Trinity Bay.

5) *Halfyard Heritage*, published by Robert R. Halfyard, 9 Frontenac Drive, St. Catherine's Ontario, L2M 2E1. The emphasis is on the name Halfyard, with those in Newfoundland coming from Ochre Pit Cove, Conception Bay. This genealogical publication brings together Halfyards from Devon, England, Newfoundland, mainland Canada and the United States. Many other names appear in the genealogies, some of which are Churchill, Carnell, Gillingham, Hooper, Parsons and Penny.

6) *The Livyere*, published twice a year by Leeward Publishing Ltd., Box 567, Gander, Newfoundland, A1V 2E1. *The Livyere* contains stories, folklore, poetry, book reviews, and some articles about family names. (Note: a "Livyere" is a resident of Newfoundland, everyone else being a "come-from-away".) The focus of this publication is on Labrador.

7) *Newfoundland Lifestyle*, published six times a year since 1983, at Box 2356, Station "C", St. John's, Newfoundland A1C 6E7. It features articles of historical and biographical interest.

8) *Newfoundland Quarterly*, published since 1901 by the Newfoundland Quarterly Foundation, Box 13486, Station "A", St. John's, Newfoundland A1B 4B8. This quarterly contains historical articles, reviews and poetry by the province's leading scholars. Each issue contains a section, "Aspects" - a publication of the Newfoundland Historical Society, edited by Dr. Leslie Harris, President of Memorial University of Newfoundland. The articles on history, culture and folklore make this a valuable publication for genealogists.

9) *Newfoundland Studies*, published twice a year since 1985 by the Department of English Language & Literature, Memorial University, St. John's, Newfoundland A1C 5S7, offers essays in the arts and sciences about the society and culture of Newfoundland, as well as reviews and bibliographies of recent publications relating to Newfoundland and Labrador.

10) *The Newfoundland Ancestor*, published quarterly by the Newfoundland and Labrador Genealogical Society since 1984, contains genealogies, charts and articles of direct benefit to the family historian. A Research Interest Section allows members of the Society to advertise their area of genealogical interest. The address of the Society is the Colonial Bld., Military Rd., St. John's, Newfoundland A1C 2C9.

11) *Them Days, Stories of Early Labrador*; Box 939, Station "B", Happy Valley, Goose Bay, Labrador, A0P 1E0. A quarterly magazine full of information for the Labradorian and his descendants, and publishes interviews about early Labrador life, culture and history. A significant archive of Labrador has been accumulated and is now being catalogued and indexed. Copies of documents, letters and early photographs add to the value of *Them Days*.

12) *The Rounder*, published 1974-1983 by the Newfoundland and Labrador Rural Development Council, contains topical articles and short historical essays of interest to and concerning rural Newfoundland. Copies are on file at the public library and should be available through the interlibrary loan system.

BIBLIOGRAPHY

Newfoundland Genealogies:

The following family histories have been published by their authors and copies donated to the Provincial Archives, the Provincial Reference and Resource Library or the genealogical society.

The Andrews Family of Cape Island and Wesleyville, by C.K. Andrews
The Baird Family of Twillingate
The Bindon Family History, by Robert Power

The Butt Family, by W. John Butt
The Coates Family, by Reginald Coates
The Cowan Family, by Frances McKinlay
The Drake Family of Catalina, Trinity Bay, by Mildred and Donald West
The Earle Genealogy
The Easterbook Family Genealogy
The Foote Family of Newfoundland, by Pat Kelley
The Fox Family
The Halfyard Genealogy, by Robert Halfyard
Adventure with John Esau Miles, by Marguerite L. Taylor
Families of the South-Arm of Bonne Bay, 1800's-1930's by Roy M. Osmond
The Reynolds Family - "The Ancestor Story and How it Grew" and "It Grew Some More", by Cecil Reynolds
From Snow to Snow, by James Snow
Genealogy of Isaac Smith of Bishop's Cove, by Clark Barrett
The Stone Heritage, by Frances Pye, Mary Graham and Lloyd Stone
The Family of William Tuff, Ochre Pit Cove, Musgrave Harbour, Bennett Island, by C.K. Andrews
The Win(d)sor Family of Greenspond, Swain's Island and Wesleyville, by C.K. Andrews

The index of the Private Papers Collection at the Provincial Archives should be checked for additional genealogies. Many families have also donated personal papers and letters to the Archives and these form some of the most interesting material in the Private Papers Collection. The index to the Private Papers may be consulted in person at the Archives, or the genealogist on staff will be able to advise you if your family name is listed in the index. Private genealogies are also located at the Centre for Newfoundland Studies, the Provincial Reference and Resource Library, or the Maritime History Archive. Not only is donating your genealogy a very nice way of thanking the institute which helped provide the information, but it also creates the opportunity for future genealogists researching the same families to read the work and contact its author.

General Reference:

Chang, Margaret. *Provincial Archives of Newfoundland - A Guide to the Government Records of Newfoundland.* St. John's, September 1983.

The Dissenting Church of Christ at St. John's 1775-1975, a history of St. David's Presbyterian Church.

Grenville, Nancy. *A Guide to the Archival Holdings of the Centre for Newfoundland Studies*, Memorial University Library. 1983.

Mannion, John (Ed.). *The Peopling of Newfoundland, Essays in Historical Geography.* St. John's, 1977.

Matthews, Keith. *Lectures on the History of Newfoundland 1500-1830*, 1988.

Matthews, Keith. *Who Was Who in Newfoundland 1660-1840.*

Neary, Peter, and Patrick O'Flaherty. *Part of the Main - An Illustrated History of Newfoundland and Labrador.* St. John's, 1983.

Researching Your Family's History in Newfoundland and Labrador. Newfoundland and Labrador Genealogical Society, 1986.

Prowse, D.W., Q.C. *A History of Newfoundland from the English, Colonial and Foreign Records.* 1895.

Rowe, Frederick W. *A History of Newfoundland and Labrador.* 1980.

Seary, E.R. *Family Names of the Island of Newfoundland.* 1977.

Smallwood, Joseph R. (Ed.). *Encyclopedia of Newfoundland and Labrador*, volumes 1 and 2. 1981.

Smith, Shelley, comp. *Provincial Archives of Newfoundland and Labrador Inventory of the Government Records Collection*, 2nd. ed., 1988.

Turk, Marion G. *The Quiet Adventurers in Canada.* Channel Island connections. 1975. (Available from Genie Repros, 4059 Commerce Ave., Cleveland, Ohio, 44130)

ACKNOWLEDGEMENTS:

Clifford Andrews, Heather Butt, Edward Chafe CG(C), Charles Cameron, Lynne Cuthbert, David Davis, Dr. Garfield Fizzard, Judy Foote, Burnham Gill, Dr. W. Gordon Handcock, Anne Hart, Philip Hiscock, Judy McGrath, Don Morris, Faith March, Margaret Mullins, Dr. Bobbie Robertson, Dr. Shannon Ryan, George Snelgrove, Dr. Gerald Thomas, Heather Wareham, Lynne West, and Lesley Winsor.

NOVA SCOTIA

by Terrence M. Punch, CG(C)

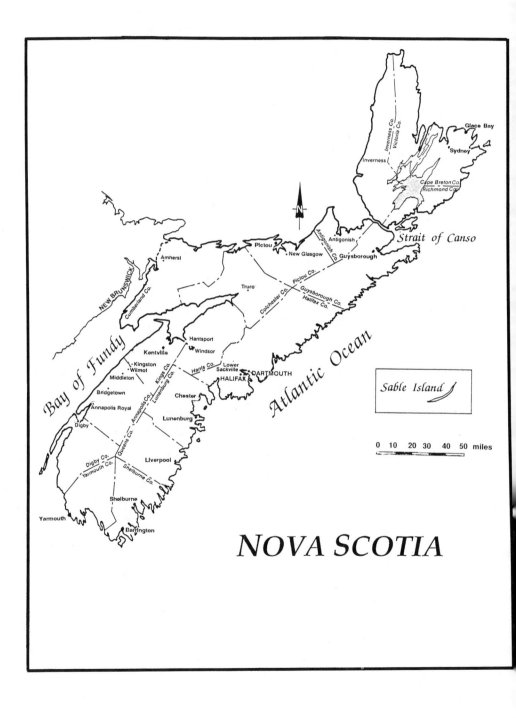

NOVA SCOTIA

HISTORICAL OVERVIEW

The province was called Acadia by the French, whose presence dates from 1605, and Nova Scotia by the British, who contested the territory for a century and a half. As a French colony administered from Port Royal (Annapolis) before 1710, Acadia was larger than the province of Nova Scotia. Under the terms of the Treaty of Utrecht (1713), mainland Acadia passed to British rule while the islands in the Gulf of St. Lawrence remained French. A major effort was made by France to develop Ile-Royale (Cape Breton) and Ile. St.-Jean (Prince Edward Island) against further British conquest. Through forty years, Britain and France argued whether the territory forming modern New Brunswick was part of Acadia. During the 1750s the British occupied all the French territory in the region, and after 1763 the entire Maritime Provinces formed part of Nova Scotia. In 1769 Prince Edward Island passed under separate administration, and in 1784 Cape Breton and New Brunswick became distinct colonies, though the former was again attached to Nova Scotia after 1820.

Despite the deportation of most of the Acadian French population in 1755-1763, the Acadians who avoided expulsion as well as those who returned from their exile in later years form the longest settled ethnic group in the province apart from the descendants of the original Micmac inhabitants. British settlement in Nova Scotia really began only with the founding of Halifax in 1749. During the following generation various elements arrived to form part of the enduring basic stock of Nova Scotia: "Foreign Protestants" from the Rhine and Montébliard, the New England planters, the Irish, and Yorkshiremen. To these were added a sizable number of Loyalists and Hessians after the American Revolution, blacks, and a large immigration of Scots.

A Legislative Assembly was established in 1758, and was accorded control over the executive branch in 1848 (responsible government). In 1867 Nova Scotia, with New Brunswick, was a founding province of the Dominion of Canada. One legacy of the time when a Scots king of England granted Nova Scotia to Sir William Alexander and his baronets is the provincial flag, the standard of St. Andrew of Scotland with its colours reversed and the royal shield of Scotland in the centre. To this day the legitimate heraldic authority for Nova Scotia is the Court of Lord Lyon in Edinburgh.

It has been reliably calculated that in addition to the nearly 900,000 people who reside in the province, another four million people live elsewhere who can trace their ancestry to one or more persons who once made their home in Nova Scotia. Likewise, the ports of Nova Scotia served as important stopping points for immigrant vessels en route from Britain and continental Europe to destinations elsewhere in North America. All in all, the records of Nova Scotia concern far more than the contemporary inhabitants of the province.

MAJOR REPOSITORY

The first provincial archivist was appointed in 1859, and the first archives building opened in 1930. The present building of the Public Archives of Nova Scotia opened in 1980. Here the genealogist will find the most comprehensive collection of primary and secondary historical material relating to Nova Scotia. The Archives, in addition to such public records as probate, land, administrative and census papers, houses the records of many societies and businesses. The P.A.N.S. incorporates within its inventory a substantial library of books, journals and newspapers. It is highly likely that any person engaged in research upon a family resident in Nova Scotia will at some point make use of the Public Archives of Nova Scotia.

The *Public Archives of Nova Scotia* (P.A.N.S.) is housed in a modern building at 6016 University Avenue (corner of Robie), Halifax, N.S. B3H 1W4. There are four public floors, with the ground floor offering a display area, the T.B. Akins meeting room, offices and a board room. The second floor is essentially a library, though microfilms of land and probate records as well as a large newspaper collection are kept here, along with the thousands of volumes of Nova Scotiana. The third floor houses most of the primary source or manuscript material, while the fifth floor (open 8:30-16:30, Monday to Friday) is occupied by the map and picture collections, and a sound archives.

The P.A.N.S. is open from 8:30-16:30, Monday, Tuesday, Wednesday, and Saturday; 8:30-22:00 Thursday and Friday. The usual civil service holidays are observed, sometimes extending into long weekends. Foreign visitors should know that three Canadian holidays differ from those in the United States: Victoria Day (one of the two last Mondays in May), Canada Day (1 July or the following Monday if the first is on a weekend), and Thanksgiving Day (the second Monday in October).

The visiting researcher begins by signing in at the security desk just inside the front entrance, and then takes the elevator to the appropriate floor. Published material, newspapers, wills or deeds are on the second floor; maps, photographs, tapes and paintings are on the fifth floor; and for almost anything else you go to the third floor.

On the second floor there is a standard library card catalogue in front of you as you step off the elevator, enabling you to locate any book or journal by author, title or subject. A librarian or assistant will be found at the counter to the right of the elevator should you need assistance. At or near that counter are the finding aids for newspapers, probate, and registry of deeds materials. The attendant will explain which type of requisition slip you must complete to obtain the item required.

On the third floor the major finding aids are the card catalogues located in a series of wooden file cabinets, and the set of black binders located in open shelving across the room from the elevator. The former are subdivided into "biography", "genealogy" and "land grant" sections on the near side, while "miscellaneous" and "communities" are on the far side. The black binders will assist the researcher by offering a catalogue or listing of the contents of each of the types of records. Modern archives divide most of their holdings into two categories - Manuscript Groups (M.G.) and Records Groups (R.G.). The former are privately-generated materials, while the latter are those created by the functions of government at any level.

To the right of the elevator on the third floor is the control desk where one or more of the helpful staff will be found on duty. Nearby are open shelves containing census, vital statistics, and some other commonly-used microfilm. These may be used, one or two at a time, without filling out a requisition slip; all other materials kept on the third floor must be requisitioned, with a limit of three items at one time.

Some of the genealogically significant M.G. materials include:

M.G.1. - papers of families and individuals (often the collections of genealogical researchers).
M.G.3. - business papers.
M.G.4. - churches and communities (described in the section "Church Records").

Also within M.G.4 are township books. These were characteristically kept by settlers from New England whose tradition of town meetings and record keeping did not survive long in Nova Scotia. However, a number of useful township books have survived, being particularly useful for the period between the late eighteenth and early nineteenth centuries. Geographically, the New England townships were located in western Nova Scotia and, with few exceptions, all township books pertain to that area. A full list with dates is given in T.M. Punch, *Genealogical Research in Nova Scotia* (Halifax: Nimbus, 1978, 1983), p. 68. The townships for which books have been filmed or the originals deposited at the P.A.N.S. are Annapolis, Argyle, Aylesford, Barrington, Chester, Cornwallis, Douglas, Falmouth, Country Harbour, Fort Lawrence, Granville, Guysborough/Manchester, Horton, Liverpool, Londonderry, Newport, Onslow, Parrsboro, Rawdon, River Philip, St. Mary's River, Truro, Westchester, Wilmot, Windsor and Yarmouth. The last-named has been published by the Yarmouth County Historical Society, Box 39, Yarmouth, N.S. B5A 4B1.

M.G.5.	cemeteries (described in the section "Cemetery Records").
M.G.15	ethnic collections (mainly Acadian, black and native people).
M.G.20	records of societies.
M.G.100	miscellaneous.

Among the R.G. materials may be mentioned the following:

R.G.5	papers of the Legislature (the petitions to government are particularly informative and should be consulted).
R.G.12	census (described in the section "Census Records").
R.G.13	customs.
R.G.14	schools (registers from 1820s to 1840s often give the child's age and father's name; school censuses of 1937 and 1946 exist but can only be consulted by a staff member on your behalf).
R.G.18	immigration and naturalization (records are skimpy and tend to be of much less assistance than the genealogist would wish).
R.G.20	land grants and petitions (described in the section "Land Records").
R.G.22	militia.
R.G.32	vital statistics (described in the section "Vital Records").
R.G.35	municipal records (assessment lists, etc., mainly since late nineteenth century.)
R.G.41	coroner's inquests and medical reports (more recent parts closed).
R.G.47	registrar of deeds (described in the section "Land Records").
R.G.48	courts of probate (described in the section "Probate Records").
R.G.49	citizenship (described in the section "Immigration").

The P.A.N.S. possesses a very good collection of older provincial, regional and urban directories. Through the use of a series of such publications a researcher may often follow the movements of families from about the 1860s. Locating street addresses about census years saves considerable time when one is seeking residents within larger towns and cities, as one is able to concentrate on the specific ward or section of town rather than having to search the entire municipality in the census returns.

Another means of locating a family, at least in the period 1864-1888, is to examine the Ambrose Church maps, a full set of which is possessed by the fifth floor of the P.A.N.S. Rural districts show every house and the name of the principal occupant. A series of insets on the maps will enable one to find the exact location of family members even within some relatively small communities.

The P.A.N.S. offers photocopying service by staff members at 25¢ per page. Visitors may photograph microfilm material for themselves on the second floor. Copying of photographs may be arranged with staff. Their telephone number is 902-424-6076.

VITAL RECORDS

In Nova Scotia, registration of birth, death and marriage by government falls into four phases:

Pre-1864   The province did not register births or deaths. Births and some deaths were entered in township books in areas for which these were kept (P.A.N.S., M.G.4). Marriages could be contracted by banns (i.e., being called several times in church) or by license. A large but incomplete collection of licenses and bonds (designed to protect women from a breach of promise of matrimony) is in the custody of the P.A.N.S. There is no general index to these available, but the staff of the Archives have put them into chronological order, which facilitates reference if one knows the approximate time of marriage. Researchers are cautioned that the existence of a license or a bond is not proof that a marriage took place.

Between 1864 and 1876 - The province of Nova Scotia commenced official registration of vital events in 1864. The thoroughness of the process and the level of public cooperation and acceptance was apparently low. Researchers cannot regard the birth and death records as complete. In 1876 the government abandoned its registration of births and deaths. Only for marriages did Nova Scotia continue unbroken such registration after 1864. Birth and death records for the twelve years, 1864-1876, with their microfilm index, are now housed in the P.A.N.S., third floor. Index reels of film are located on an open shelf in the third floor reading room. Surnames and locations found in these birth records are listed and classified by T.M. Punch in *In Which County? Nova Scotia Surnames from Birth Registers; 1864 to 1877* (Halifax: Genealogical Association of Nova Scotia, 1985).

Users of birth registrations can expect to find the place and date of birth, the child's name, and that of its parents. It is good practice to verify dates and details by finding the appropriate record of christening in church whenever possible. Users of death registers will find the date and place of death, the name and age of decedents, their birthplace, cause of death and (occasionally for adults) parents' names. Again, researchers are advised to corroborate as many of the particulars as possible through newspaper obituaries and cemetery inscriptions. Marriage records from 1864 into the twentieth century are the most informative and useful for genealogical purposes. From them one will learn the date and place of marriage, the name and denomination of the officiant, the names, ages, marital status and residence of both married parties, his trade or profession, their parents' names and trades, and the names of the witnesses.

Between 1877 and 1908 - In all essential respects, Nova Scotia's birth and death registration during these thirty years reverted to its pre-1864 condition, i.e., nonexistent. Mitigating this circumstance is the fact that by 1877 there were more and better kept church records, and the further fact that more headstones survive from this later period than from the earlier one. Marriage records continued to be kept from 1864 to 1876, and are available for consultation at the P.A.N.S. to about 1910 (R.G. 32, Series "M"). The cutoff dates by counties are: 1906-Guysborough; 1908 - Annapolis, Inverness, Lunenburg, Shelburne, Yarmouth; 1909 - Digby, Kings; 1910 - Antigonish, Queens; 1912 - Cape Breton; 1913 - Cumberland; 1914 - Colchester; 1916 - Halifax, Hants; 1917 - Pictou; 1918 - Richmond, Victoria.

Since 1908   Marriage records continued unchanged from the previous period in terms of information gathered, but the registers and their indexes are not held at P.A.N.S. More recent marriage registrations, together with birth and death records, which resumed on 1 October 1908, are in the custody of the Deputy Registrar-General, P.O. Box 157, Halifax, N.S., B3J 2M9, telephone 902-424-4374.

The Registrar must be told the name, date and location of any marriage, birth or death for which record is sought. You must state that you want the certification for genealogical purposes. If you do not know the exact date, the Registrar will make a search through three years (the year you mention and that on either side of it) for $2.00. If the entry is found that fee becomes part of the certificate fee. Otherwise, the fee is simply retained by the office. The Registrar will not send enquirers a listing of all the entries for a given surname, simply because this would necessitate a lengthy hand search for which they lack sufficient staff. The fee for a short form certificate is $5.00, while that for the long form is $10.00. The Registrar will accept a postal money order in Canadian funds, but personal cheques must be stated in the correct exact prices as shown above, and no indication may be written on the cheque to specify currency ("Canadian", "American"). The public cannot search indexes in the Registrar's office, nor is it customary practice to issue death certificates on which the cause of death is given.

CENSUS RECORDS

The population returns of Nova Scotia fall into three classifications, based on whether the census information was gathered by officials of the French, colonial or Canadian governments. Briefly described, the French era in mainland Nova Scotia ended about 1713, and in Cape Breton Island in 1758. The several population returns from the French period are listed and described in the chapter regarding the Centre d'Études acadiennes.

The first return of people in British colonial Nova Scotia is that made for Halifax and vicinity in the summer of 1752. Only heads of family are named, a characteristic of all census returns for the colonial period. The remaining members of the household are represented merely by numbers under the headings: males over 16, females over 16, males below 16, females below 16, total number. This return is printed as an appendix to Akins' "History of Halifax City" which forms volume eight of the *Collections* of the Nova Scotia Historical Society.

Between 1770 and 1787 seventeen townships or counties were recorded, the customary format being: 1. name of head of household, 2. numbers in the household (men, boys, women, girls), 3. total number of persons, 4. religion (Protestant or Roman Catholic), and 5. country (English, Scots, Irish, German, American, Acadian). The 1770-1787 returns have been published twice, once as appendix B to the 1934 annual report of the P.A.N.S., and again, with index, by the Chicago Genealogical Society, under the title *Nova Scotia 1770 Census*.

Chronologically the next censuses were taken on Cape Breton Island. Abbé François Lejamtel listed the people in his territory in 1797 (lost) and 1809. The latter, covering Chéticamp and Margaree, is transcribed in Anselme Chiasson's *Chéticamp: Histoire et Traditions acadiennes*, pp. 291-295. Parts of all four Cape Breton counties are represented in the 1811 census (headings: head of family, occupation, age and sex, cattle, etc., stations [location]). The surviving portions of the 1818 census (headings: heads of family, age, time on the island, country, country of parents, location, trade, marital status, number of children) are printed, together with the 1811 material, as appendix A to *Holland's Description of Cape Breton Island* (Halifax: P.A.N.S., 1935).

A provincial census of mainland Nova Scotia in 1817 is largely lost, but the portions representing the modern counties of Hants, Antigonish, Pictou and Guysborough have survived, as well as those for the St. Margaret's Bay area of Halifax and Lunenburg counties. Abbé J.-M. Sigogne compiled lists of his parishioners at Ste. Anne and St. Pierre (Argyle area, Yarmouth County) in 1816-1819, and at Baie-Ste.-Marie (Digby County) in 1818-19 and 1840-44.

The 1827 census asked each head of household for the numbers in his family, their sex, his occupation and religion, and the number of births, deaths or marriages occurring in the household within the preceding twelvemonth. Most of the surviving portions of the 1827 census, together with that of Pictou for 1817/18, were published by the P.A.N.S. The Antigonish County portion was published as appendix B to the 1938 annual report of the P.A.N.S.

The earliest census to survive almost in its entirety is that of 1838, which lacks most of Cumberland County. The returns give names of heads of family only, together with an age-sex breakdown of the household, occupation and total. It is useful in locating a family within the province at the height of the colonial era. The 1838 census has yet to be published. The next census, that of 1851, gives a more sophisticated age-sex breakdown and adds a column for religion, but has survived (apparently) for just the counties of Halifax, Hants and Pictou (P.A.N.S., R.G. 1, Vols, 451, 452).

The 1861 returns are the earliest to survive for the entire province and the last to be taken by the colonial authorities of the province. Its personal data is much the same as that for the 1851 returns, but there is considerable additional information about what each household grew/made/produced.

The federal Canadian census of 1871, like its counterparts for 1881 and 1891, is available on microfilm for consultation. It is a goldmine since it gives a wide variety of data about each individual person in the whole province. One can learn name, sex, age, country of birth, religion, ethnic origin, occupation, marital status, literacy, and handicaps from these returns.

One should augment the census returns by reference to the card index of various poll tax lists of the 1790s. These lists cover most of the settled portions of mainland Nova Scotia at that time, but not, however, Dartmouth, Clare, Granville, Kempt and Parrsboro. Another method of adding to location records of this type is to examine lists of inhabitants of the various areas for which a local or county history has been published. Calnek's *History of Annapolis County*, for example, gives lists of settlers in the military settlements at Dalhousie and vicinity.

Census returns are excellent locational records, but tend to be less than totally reliable as sources for ages or relationships among listed persons. Researchers into Nova Scotian family history would be well advised to corroborate census data in general.

LAND RECORDS

Records of land acquisition and ownership fall logically into two parts, those which relate to the original granting of lands, and those which form the legal record of land ownership and transferral since the initial grants.

Land Grants

The readiest access to the largest number of land grants is through the P.A.N.S., where grants and petitions for land are filed under R.G.20. There is a large alphabetical file that indexes draft land grants and petitions which ask for land. Series "A", covering the entire province, is filed in two parts, with 1800 as the dividing date. Series "B", 1787-1848, pertains specifically to Cape Breton Island, and forms a large typescript available to patrons on the third floor of P.A.N.S.

Many petitions recite information about the petitioner's family, place of origin, date of immigration, military experience and whatever else the petitioner thought might give him a claim on the bounty of the government. In many cases, especially when grants of land were made to large groups of people, the grant itself need not imply settlement or occupation. One should also examine allotment or township records for evidence of use or transferral. For Loyalists and some few others, researchers should consult Marion Gilroy, *Loyalists and Land Settlement in Nova Scotia* (Halifax: P.A.N.S., 1937; reprinted, with surname index, by the Genealogical Committee in 1980). Here one will find that many grants were escheated (i.e. taken back by the government) because the conditions of the grant, such as settlement or development, were not being met.

The Crown Lands Office, Dept. of Lands and Forests, 1740 Granville St., Halifax, N.S. B3J 1X5, telephone 902-424-3179, has a set of 140 maps showing the first grants in each district, on a scale of one inch to 80 chains (which, at 66 feet to the surveyor's chain, comes out to 1"=1 mile). If you locate a grant geographically, you may be able to obtain a map showing the grant and the adjacent area. The cost is $2.20 per map from the Crown Lands Office. P.A.N.S. also has a set of these maps as well as a microfilm index of land grants that spans over 200 years.

Registries of Deeds

Subsequent to the land grants and any escheats and regrants, the preservation of land records became the responsibility of the municipalities (counties or rural municipalities). The land registry, or Registry of Deeds, comprehends a mass of mortgages, deeds, leases and releases, liens, sheriff's deeds, orders of the court, and some wills which bequeathed real estate. Technically each instrument by which ownership is transferred is supposed to be registered, though obviously they have not always been recorded. Many land records include plans or maps of premises or larger areas. Some plans show persons of the same surname upon adjacent lands, and these may be co-heirs of the first grantee. In areas where some surnames are very common, such a clue to kinship will be critical to the genealogist.

Deeds require an index to grantors (lessor, vendor, or seller) and another to grantees (leasee, emport, or purchaser). Some indexes indicate the year and location of lands that the transaction affects; some indicate the type of instrument. The transactors' names may be followed by a code that indicates whether or not he acted alone. Some deeds were made *et ux.* (with wife) or *et al.* (with others), or as the trustee or attorney of someone else. Seachers should, of course, check indexes under spelling variants and possible translations (e.g. White for LeBlanc).

Land office records in Nova Scotia are held in the Registries of Deeds of the several counties and districts, as well as at P.A.N.S. for those prior to the early twentieth century. Typically a Registry of Deeds charges a nominal fee of a dollar or two per day to admit researchers. For those, such as visitors who do not have time to visit several court houses or municipal buildings where land transaction records are held, the P.A.N.S. will be a convenient one-stop location in which to search transactions between 1749 and about 1910. The following is a list of counties and municipalities possessing land records, together with the inclusive dates of microfilmed land records in the custody of the P.A.N.S.

The archives comprehends all of this material within its R.G. 47, as follows:

County: Subdivision	Date of Formation	Deed Dates Held	Remarks on the County or Municipality
Annapolis	1759	1763-1910	Formerly part of Hfx.
Antigonish	1784	1785-1907	Formerly part of Hfx.
Cape Breton	1784	1786-1910	Separate government to 1820; county since
Colchester	1835	1770-1903	Formerly a district of Hfx. County
Cumberland	1759		Formerly part of Hfx. County
Amherst		1764-1904	Responsible for northern and eastern area
Parrsboro		1789-1905	Responsible for the south-western district
Digby	1837	1785-1910	Formerly part of Annapolis County
Guysborough	1836		Formerly part of Hfx. County
Guysborough		1785-1910	Responsible for eastern half of county
Sherbrooke		1815-1910	Responsible for western half of county
Halifax	1749	1749-1903	The original jurisdiction
Hants	1781	1763-1906	Formerly part of Kings County
Inverness	1835	1825-1910	Formerly part of Cape Breton County
Kings	1759		Formerly part of Hfx. County
Aylesford		1820-1843	Jurisdiction removed to Kentville
Cornwallis		1764-1903	Cornwallis records at Kentville
Horton		1766-1843	Jurisdiction removed to Kentville
Lunenburg	1759		Formerly part of Halifax
Chester		1879-1908	Responsible for eastern county areas
Lunenburg		1759-1912	Responsible for central and western county
Pictou	1835	1771-1905	Formerly a district of Hfx. County
Queens	1762	1764-1920	Formerly part of Lunen-burg County

Richmond	1835	1821-1909	Formerly part of Cape Breton County
Shelburne	1784		Formerly part of Queens County
Barrington		1854-1913	Responsible for western part of county
Shelburne		1783-1921	Responsible for eastern part of county
Victoria	1851	1851-1911	Formerly part of Cape Breton County
Yarmouth	1836	1766-1910	Formerly part of Shelburne County

Antigonish and Guysborough together formed Sydney County between 1784 and 1836, and readers ought not to confuse the *county* of Sydney with the town and city located on Cape Breton Island. For two years between its formation and 1837, Inverness was known as Juste au Corps County and a few records may be seen using that designation. Nova Scotia has also a "lost" county, that of Sunbury; in 1784 Sunbury and other areas were detached from Nova Scotia to form the province of New Brunswick. Researchers should also know that the municipality of Clare forms part of Digby County, and that of St. Mary's is the area of Guysborough County included under Sherbrooke. Finally, the Parrsboro area was included within Kings County until 1840, when most of it was assigned to Cumberland County, though a portion was added to Colchester County as well. These divisions and subdivisions are set forth by C.B. Fergusson in *The Boundaries of Nova Scotia and its Counties* (Halifax: P.A.N.S., 1966).

Genealogical researchers will derive benefit also from the series of maps drawn by Ambrose Church to show every house in each county. Householders' names are given (but often misspelled) by each property. Insets show towns and many villages, house by house. Copies may be obtained for a few dollars each from the Dept. of Lands and Forests, Box 698, Halifax, N.S. B3J 2T9, or from Maritime Resources Management Service, Box 310, Amherst, N.S. B4H 3Z5. In order of appearance, the maps are Halifax, 1865, Pictou 1867, Yarmouth & Digby 1870, Hants 1871, Kings 1872, Cumberland 1873, Colchester 1874, Guysborough & Annapolis 1876, Cape Breton 1877, Antigonish 1878, Shelburne 1882, Inverness, Lunenburg, Richmond & Victoria 1883-1887, and Queens 1888. Users should expect that the data on any of Church's maps may have been collected between one and several years prior to the indicated date.

PROBATE RECORDS

Probate registration began formally in Nova Scotia in 1749 with the settlement of Halifax. Twenty jurisdictions now operate within the province. The nature of records generated by the probating of an estate depend upon whether the deceased person made a will (was testate), or had left no testamentary writing (was intestate).

A will must be "proved", which means that those who witnessed its signing satisfy the court that the will is what it is claimed to be. There may be additions made to the will after it was signed and these additions are called codicils and form part of the total will for purposes of probate, although in the files they will probably be on separate sheets of paper and bear a different date from the will. In earlier times, when death records may be incomplete, the death of a testator can be established as falling between the latest date on his will or codicil(s) and the earliest date of the will's presentation to the probate court. Customarily in Nova Scotia, all wills proved in a given jurisdiction were "entered", i.e., written into the will registers of that county. These registers have been microfilmed and may be consulted at the P.A.N.S., where they form R.G. 48.

A further series of probate records form the documentation for intestate estates and the auxiliary documentation connected with the probate of a will. Here one will find letters of administration, requests for such letters, inventories of the property -- real and personal-- of the estate, and much other incidental legal paperwork, accounts of executors, etc. These may be termed original estate papers. Below is a list of P.A.N.S. holdings in this regard. More recent material and perhaps other documentation must be sought at the several probate courts around the province.

County: Subdivision	Will Dates	Original Estate Papers Dates
Annapolis	1879-1970	1763-1900
Antigonish	1821-1963	1819-1900
Cape Breton	1802-1969	1782-1902
Colchester	1770-1969	1800-1900
Cumberland	1796-1969	1764-1900
Digby	1810-1970	
Guysborough		
Guysborough	1942-1967	
Sherbrooke	1843-1969	
Halifax	1749-1903	1749-1871

Hants	1761-1968	
Inverness	1831-1969	1830-1906
Kings	1783-1968	
Lunenburg	1762-1967	
Pictou	1811-1969	1813-1901
Queens	1768-1970	1765-1901
Richmond	1831-1913	
	1941-1969	
Shelburne		
Shelburne	1785-1970	1766-1900
Barrington	1868-1969	1784-1900
Victoria	1856-1968	1852-1901
Yarmouth	1794-1970	1794-1900

Researchers should not neglect the Halifax County original estate papers in their search for documentation in other jurisdictions. Prior to about 1842, much of the material one would expect to find under the appropriate county will appear at the end of each letter of the alphabet following the Halifax documentation. Most of these documents pertain to "insolvent estates"- those where a sale of real property had to be ordered to discharge the indebtedness of the deceased.

CHURCH RECORDS

Since civil registration, except for marriages, scarcely existed in Nova Scotia before 1908, church registers of births / baptisms, deaths / burials and marriage assume primary importance for the genealogist. The registers listed below are held on microfilm at the P.A.N.S. and may usually be consulted freely, with the important exception of most of the Anglican records, for which the prior permission of the pastor or bishop is required. The selection below lists only churches whose records antedate 1908. (**A** Anglican; **B** Baptist; **C** Catholic; **Cong** Congregationalist; **L** Lutheran; **M** Methodist; **P** Presbyterian; **U** United)

Annapolis Co:	Annapolis Royal	A	1782-1950
		C	1702-1755
		M/P/U	1834-1984
	Bridgetown	M	1793-1969
		A	1830-1969
	Clementsport	A	1841-1973
	Granville	A	1790-1801, 1814-1918
		M	1824-1831
	Melvern Square	B	1870-1890
	Middleton	U	1858-1958

	Rosette	A	1891-1956
	Wilmot	A	1789-1973
Antigonish Co:	Antigonish	A	1829-1976
		U	1854-1962
	Arisaig	C	1845-1921
	Lochaber	P	1811-1944
Cape Breton Co:	Dominion	A	1906-1973
	Donkin	P/U	1900-1966
	East Bay	C	1860-1908
	Gabarus	M	1867-1908
	Glace Bay	U	1903-1963
	Grand Mira	C	1845-1981
	Ile-Royale	C	1715-1721, 1726-1749, 1753-1757
	Louisbourg	C	1722-1745, 1749-1758
	Marion Bridge	M/U	1867-1980
	New Waterford	A	1918-1969
		P/U	1918-1969
	North Sydney	A	1882-1984
		M/U	1884-1981
	Port Morien	A	1865-1971
		P	1900-1903, 1910-1970
	Sydney	A	1785-1981
		C	1833-1840, 1846-1869 (Sacred Heart)
		M	1903-1937
		P	1815-1981 (Saint Andrew's)
		U	1882-1918 (First)
	Sydney Mines	A	1816, 1848-1970
		C	1884-1978
	Victoria Mines	C	1856-1975
Colchester Co:	Earltown	P	1782-1966
	Economy	U	1871-1964
	Glenholme	U	1892-1956
	Great Village	P/U	1852-1872 1876-1982
	Harmony	A	1887-1953
	Londonderry	A	1865-1964
	Londonderry	C	1878-1909
		M/U	1870-1949
		P	1795-1835
	Lower Stewiacke	A	1850-1963

	Old Barns	U	1908-1979
	Stewiacke	U	1893-1956
	Tatamagouche	M	1855-1956
		P	1853-1931
	Truro	A	1824-1967
		C	1873-1891, 1894-1909
		P	1834-1854
		U	1873-1979 (First)
	Upper Londonderry	U	1859-1965
	Upper Stewiacke	P	1872-1969
	Valley	P	1872-1972 (Coldstream)
Cumberland Co:	Amherst	A	1822-1965
		C	1888-1909
		M/U	1912-1984
		P	1840-1970
	Beaubassin	C	1679-1686, 1712-1748
	Joggins	A	1898-1976
		C	1848-1909
	Oxford	M	1883-1903
	Parrsboro	A	1787-1972
		C	1853-1909
		M	1853-1972
		P	1858-1972
	Port Greville	A	1897-1969
		M	1899-1972
	Pugwash	A	1849-1980
		M	1875-1958
		P	1857-1895, 1906-1941
	Remsheg/Wallace	A	1832-1926
		M	1831-1927
	Southampton	M	1883-1968
	Springhill	A	1881-1962
		C	1897-1909
		M/U	1877-1983
	Westmorland (NB)	A	1790-1917 (Tignish: Fort Lawrence)
Digby Co:	Clements	A	1841-1973
	Digby	A	1786-1950
		P	1870-1922 (Bay View)
	Digby Neck	M	1894-1937
	Weymouth	A	1823-1948

Guysborough Co:	Canso	A	1886-1970
	Country Harbour	A	1851-1949
	Dorchester	P	1821-1853
	Guysborough	A	1786-1880
		M	1825-1907
		U	1874-1966
	Halfway Cove	A	1880-1905
	Liscomb	A	1852-1958
	Manchester	A	1847-1904
	Medford/Mulgrave	A	1854-1924
	New Harbour	U	1854-1924
	Queensport	A	1905-1942
	Sherbrooke	U	1892-1981
Halifax City:	Brunswick Street	M	1784-1979
	City Mission	M	1855-1868
	Chalmers	P	1893-1916
	Coburg Road	M	1885-1924
	Dutch Church	L/A	1783-1806
	Emmanuel	A	1893-1979 (Spryfield)
	Fort Massey	P	1875-1970
	Grafton Street	M	1856-1925
	Park Street	P	1891-1918
	Poplar Grove	P	1843-1891
	St. Agnes	C	1892-1919
	St. Andrew's	P/U	1818-1979
	St. George's	A	1813-1954
	St. John's	P/U	1843-1972
	St. Joseph's	C	1869-1909
	St. Luke's	A	1858-1910
	St. Mark's	A	1861-1965
	St. Mary's	C	1800-1909 (formerly St. Peter's)
	St. Matthew's	P/U	1769-1936
	St. Matthias	A	1888-1973
	St. Patrick's	C	1848-1854, 1879-1909
	St. Paul's	A	1749-1954
	Salem	Cong	1868-1876
	Tabernacle	B	1890-1899
	Trinity	A	1876-1983
	United Memorial	U	1890-1982
	Universalist		1852-1903
	Wesley Smith	M/U	1882-1980

Halifax Co:	Dartmouth	A	1793-1966 (Christ Church)
		C	1830-1909 (St. Peter's)
		M	1864-1977
		P	1833-1850, 1857-1976 (St. James)
	East Chezzetcook	C	1868-1909
	Eastern Passage	A	1867-1981
	Falkland	A	1877-1977
	French Village	A	1834-1963
	Goodwood	U	1954-1967
	Herring Cove	C	1837-1852, 1856-1909
	Hubbards	A	1858-1967
	Jeddore	A	1868-1953
	Ketch Harbour	C	1837-1843, 1856-1935
	Middle Musquodoboit	M	1860-1943
		P	1848-1943
	Musquodoboit Harbour	A	1894-1980
	North Beaverbank	P	1886-1964
	Port Dufferin	A	1847-1986
	Prospect	C	1823-1909
	Sackville	A	1813-1918
		U	1964-1985
	St. Margaret's Bay	M	1820-1829, 1873-1965
	Seaforth	A	1865-1945 (Porters Lake)
	Sheet Harbour	C	1857-1909
		U	1870-1979
	Ship Harbour	A	1841-1982
	Upper Musquodoboit	U	1882-1968
	Waverley	A	1920-1966
	West Chezzetcook	C	1785-1890
Hants Co:	Centre Rawdon	A	1793-1952
	Elmsdale	P	1879-1959 (Nine Mile River)
	Enfield	C	1857-1909
	Falmouth	A	1793-1934
	Hantsport	A	1892-1967
	Kennetcook	P	1876-1893
	Lakelands	A	1858-1959
	McPhee Corner	A	1860-1892
	Maitland	A	1856-1971
		M	1831-1916

	Milford	U	1870-1978 (Gays River)
	Newport/Walton	A	1793-1955
		M/P	1824-1844, 1859-1876, 1893-1926
	Rawdon	A	1793-1955
	Shubenacadie	M	1870-1912
		A	1817-1912
	West Gore	Ch. of Christ	1922-1962
	Windsor	A	1775-1795 (Fort Edward)
		A	1811-1948
		C	1834-1840, 1845-1909
		M	1898-1940
		P	1873-1963
Inverness Co:	Mabou	P/U	1886-1948
	Malagawatch	P	1882-1923
	Margaree	Cong/U	1823-1959
	Port Hastings	U	1852-1939
	Port Hawkesbury	U	1829-1978
	Port Hood	M	1877-1926
	Strathlorne	P	1894-1907
	Whycocomagh	P	1868-1978 (Stewart Church)
Kings Co:	Aylesford	A	1789-1950
	Berwick	A	1900-1930
		M/U	1864-1876
	Canning	M	1856-1962
	Cornwallis	A	1775-1969
		B	1804-1822, 1855-1875
		M	1815-1905
	Grand Pré	C	1707-1748
		U	1819-1905
	Horton/Wolfville	A	1823-1968
	Kentville	A	1893-1968
	Kings County	M	1819-1905
	Kingsport	Cong	1863-1948
	Pleasant Valley	B	1837-1857
	Upper Canard	P	1893-1962
Lunenburg Co:	Bakers Settlement	L	1899-1945
	Blandford	A	1859-1929
	Bridgewater	A	1854-1937
		C	1851-1909

Bridgewater	L	1854-1942
	U	1884-1943
Camperdown	L	1889-1946
Chester	A	1762-1801, 1812-1963
	Cong	1762-1785
Conquerall Bank	L	1889-1946
Feltzen South	L	1887-1947
Hemford	L	1888-1958
Lapland	L	1904-1946
Lunenburg	A	1753-1942
	B	1795-1858
	L	1772-1915
	M	1815-1837
	P	1770-1969
Mahone Bay	A	1845-1972
Middle Lehave	L	1887-1944 (Rose Bay)
Midville Branch	L	1889-1970
Newburn	L	1888-1952
Newcombville	L	1906-1969
New Dublin	A	1830-1850, 1867-1970
New Germany	A	1888-1973
	B	1864-1880
	L	1900-1952
New Ross	A	1822-1943
North River	L	1899-1953
Petite Riviere	U	1847-1959
Riverport	U	1881-1943
Upper Lahave	A	1884-1964
Upper Northfield	L	1901-1952
West Northfield	L	1888-1953
Waterloo	L	1880-1945

Pictou Co:	Barneys River	P	1812-1883
	Blue Mountain	P	1844-1975
	Caribou River	U	1888-1950
	Gairlock	P	1833-1977
	Greenhill	P	1833-1977
	McLellan's Mtn.	P	1838-1907
	New Glasgow	A	1888-1969
		B	1874-1960
		P	1786-1815, 1832-1908 (St. James)
		P	1908-1972 (First)
	Pictou	A	1830-1944
		M	1872-1980
		P	1824-1908 (Prince St.)

	Pictou	P	1850-1950 (Knox: First)
		P	1851-1980 (St. Andrew's)
	Pictou County	P	1817-1865
	River John	M	1855-1956
	Rogers Hill	P	1855-1907
	Scotsburn	P	1866-1980
	Stellarton	A	1851-1975 (Albion Mines)
		U	1860-1972
	West Branch, East River	P	1827-1980 (Hopewell)
	West River	P	1858-1879
	Westville	A	1897-1958
Queens Co:	Caledonia	A	1856-1962
		C	1840-1909
	Eagle Head	A	1866-1965
	Liverpool	A	1819-1976
		B	1821-1870
		C	1832-1892
		Cong	1792-1830, 1849-1851, 1874-1926
	Milton	Cong	1854-1924
	Port Mouton	U	1849-1961
Richmond Co:	Arichat	A	1828-1957
	Forchu	C	1741-1749
	Framboise	P	1888-1905
	Loch Lomond	P	1888-1972
	West Bay	P	1834-1975
Shelburne Co:	Barrington	A	1861-1867
		B	1851-1866
		M	1790-1971
	Lockeport	A	1883-1974
		U	1894-1974
	Northeast Harbour	U	1878-1965
	Roseway	A	1885-1922
	Sable River	B	1841-1966
	Shelburne	A	1783-1971
		M	1790-1821, 1856-1926
		P/U	1828-1954
Victoria Co:	Baddeck	A	1877-1927

	Boularderie	P	1906-1966
	Ingonish	M	1874-1965
	Neil's Harbour	A	1876-1984
Yarmouth Co:	Chebogue	Cong	1769-1785
	Eel Brook	C	1799-1841 (Tusket)
	Yarmouth	A	1898-1973
		P	1849-1899

Church Repositories

Many church registers are not available at the P.A.N.S. Several of the principal denominations have central offices to which the researcher is directed for advice and perhaps for permission to use registers either at the P.A.N.S. or in the custody of the various church bodies.

The Church of England in Canada (Anglican) combines Nova Scotia and Prince Edward Island within the one diocese of Nova Scotia. A diocesan archives is situated at 5732 College St., Halifax, N.S. B3H 1X3. Although the holdings of parish registers are minimal, this office can supply the names and addresses of the many rectors in the diocese, and the bishop may be contacted through this address by those hoping to obtain permission to view confidential records held by the P.A.N.S.

The Baptist records have to some extent been placed in the Maritime Baptist Archives, Vaughan Library, Acadia University, Wolfville, N.S. B0P 1X0. Examples of early records kept at the Vaughan Library include Cornwallis (1778-1806), Onslow (1791-1869), Scotch Village (1799-1911) and Weymouth North (1809-1867). Also genealogically valuable is the Archives' publication series, "Baptist Heritage in Atlantic Canada." This series began in 1979 with *The Diary of Joseph Dimock*, edited by George E. Levy, which lists the 275 marriages performed by this clergyman, mostly in Chester, between 1794 and 1845.

There are three presbyteries of the Presbyterian Church within the province:

Presbytery of Cape Breton, Box 184, Baddeck, N.S. B0E 1B0.

Presbytery of Pictou, 139 Almont Ave., New Glasgow, N.S. B2H 3G8.

Presbytery of Halifax & Lunenburg, 67 Russell St., Dartmouth, N.S. B3A 3N2.

The first covers the four island counties, the second the northern and eastern mainland, and the third the central and western mainland.

The United Church of Canada was formed by the union of most Presbyterian, Methodist and Congregationalist churches in 1925/26. Its Maritime Conference Archives are located at 640 Franklyn St., Halifax, N.S. B3J 3B5. Their holdings of registers is slight, but the archives can supply the names and addresses of local clergy.

The Roman Catholic Church in Nova Scotia is divided into three dioceses. The metropolitan see of Halifax extends to the counties of Cumberland, Colchester, Hants, Halifax, Lunenburg and Queens. Its address is Box 1527, Halifax, N.S. B3J 2Y3. The diocese of Yarmouth contains the counties of Shelburne, Yarmouth, Digby, Annapolis and Kings. The address is 43 Albert St., Yarmouth, N.S. B5A 3N1. The diocese of Antigonish extends to all of Cape Breton Island and the three eastern mainland counties of Guysborough, Antigonish and Pictou. The address is Box 1060, Antigonish, N.S. B2G 2L7. Policy concerning church registers varies by diocese: Halifax has opened everything until 1909 and most of their records have been microfilmed and may be seen at the P.A.N.S.; Antigonish has little in the way of centralized registers, so one must deal with individual parishes; Yarmouth's registers have been closed due to the unauthorized publication of information a few years ago, and permission of the bishop or parish priest is now required.

CEMETERY RECORDS

Inscriptions from a large number of the burial grounds in Nova Scotia have been transcribed and copies of most of this work have been deposited in the P.A.N.S. or one of the local historical or genealogical society collections. There is some material from the period prior to 1800, mostly from graveyards in the western mainland and in a few of the older cities and towns. Many of the stones from the period 1800-1850 have weathered badly and may be difficult or even impossible to read. Because of the difficulty of reading stones accurately, and because so much of the information placed on stones was based on memory some years after a death, headstones are better regarded as clues than taken as literal and reliable statements of fact. Only in the absence of corroborating documentation should a headstone inscription be used as the primary source of information for anyone prior to 1850.

P.A.N.S., M.G.5 is entitled *Cemeteries*. Organized by county, the most comprehensive transcriptions cover Halifax, Lunenburg, Queens, Shelburne, Annapolis, Kings, Colchester and Pictou counties. Considerable work has also been undertaken in Yarmouth, Hants and Cumberland counties. Material from other parts of the province is best sought in the local repositories of those areas.

Some transcriptions have been indexed and published. The North Cumberland Historical Society has read many cemeteries in its area and published the results in volume three of their publications series. Burials in Horton Township, Kings County, have been published by Douglas Eagles. The stones of Lunenburg, Queens and Shelburne counties have been published as *Cemetery Inscriptions for Lunenburg-Queens-Shelburne Counties*, Vols. 1-3 by the South Shore Genealogical Society.

IMMIGRATION & CITIZENSHIP

Until 1947, people from the British Isles who settled in Nova Scotia were not required to become citizens since they shared British citizenship with Canadians. Therefore, the few early naturalization records concern largely Americans and people from continental Europe. P.A.N.S., R.G. 49 (Citizenship Records) is thus a relatively small series. Until 1901, all Nova Scotian cases are on record in Halifax. Beginning at various dates, other jurisdictions were established at Digby (1901), Shelburne (1903), Lunenburg and Kentville (1916), Pictou (1918) and Truro (1922). There may be other courts with jurisdiction in these matters, but their records are not available in Nova Scotia.

Large numbers of people, particularly from the British Isles and the Rhine, were transported to Nova Scotia between 1749 and 1848. Ships, by year and port, for which passenger lists are available in print, are themselves listed in Terrence M. Punch, *Genealogical Research in Nova Scotia* (Halifax; Petheric Press, 1978, 1983), pp. 81-82. To these may be added: 1817 "William Tell", bringing Scots from Greenock, Scotland, to Sydney, N.S.; 1823 "Cumberland", bringing Irish from Waterford, Ireland, to Halifax, N.S.; 1830 "Malory", bringing Scots from the Isle of Skye to Cape Breton Island.

An overview of the subject may be obtained by reading J.S. Martell's study, *Immigration to and Emigration from Nova Scotia 1815-1838* (Halifax: P.A.N.S., 1942), and Mrs. R.G. Flewelling's continuation for 1839-1851 in the *Collections* of the Nova Scotia Historical Society, Vol. XXVIII.

NEWSPAPERS

Newspapers in Canada began at Halifax in March 1752 with the first issue of *The Gazette*. Specific coverage of deaths or marriages did not begin until the late 1760s, while nothing resembling thorough reporting of births existed until well into the nineteenth century. Social standing, ethnicity, religious affiliation and geographical location all played their parts in determining which events were reported in the press. Officials, professionals, clergy and officers enjoyed a significantly better chance of coverage than did labourers and farmers. One may observe a gradual "democratization" of reportage during the nineteenth century. Yet, along with church registers, newspapers are a major source of linkage data for Nova Scotian genealogy prior to government registration of vital statistics and the nominal census.

Unusually for a provincial archives, the P.A.N.S. actively attempts to maintain and extend a major collection of newspapers published within Nova Scotia. In order of earliest dates, some of the major holdings are:

The Gazette (and its various changes of name), Halifax, 1752-present.

The Journal, Halifax, 1781-1799, 1810-1854.

The Weekly Chronicle, Halifax, 1786-1826.

The Acadian Recorder, Halifax, 1813-1930.

The Free Press, Halifax, 1816-1848 (called *The Times* after 1834.)

The Novascotian, Halifax, 1824-1926.

The Acadian & General Advertiser, Halifax, 1827-1834.

Colonial Patriot, Pictou, 1827-1834.

Pictou Observer & Eastern Advertiser, Pictou, 1831-1835, 1838-1843.

Yarmouth Herald & Western Advertiser, Yarmouth, 1833-

The Bee, Pictou, 1835-1838.

The Pearl, Halifax, 1837-1840.

Mechanic and Farmer Pictou, 1838-1843.

Spirit of the Times & Cape Breton Free Post, Sydney, 1841-1850.

Morning News, Halifax, 1842-1846.

Eastern Chronicle, Pictou, 1843-1953.

The Morning Chronicle, Halifax, 1844-1949.

The Sun, Halifax, 1845-1867.

The British Colonist, Halifax, 1848-1874.

Numbers of denominational newspapers also appeared in the province after 1835, and these are described in T.M. Punch, *Genealogical Research in Nova Scotia* (Halifax: Nimbus, 1978, 1983), pp. 52-53. The standard reference work concerning the entire subject is the survey done by Gertrude Tratt, which is listed in the bibliography at the end of this chapter.

A continuing series of publications available from the Genealogical Association of Nova Scotia compiles and indexes the deaths, marriages and births in early provincial newspapers. To date, eight volumes have appeared and cover the years between 1769 and 1851. These may be ordered from the Genealogical Association, Box 641, Station "M", Halifax, N.S. B3J 2T3.

LIBRARIES & SOCIETIES

There is a wealth of heritage-related activity in Nova Scotia; the list presented here is at best a selection of active organizations. The area telephone code is 902. Each institution is given with address and telephone number to facilitate communication. The list is divided into those bodies having provincial, regional or municipal scope.

PROVINCIAL

Acadia University Library
Wolfville, N.S.
BOP 1X0
(phone 542-2201)

Black Cultural Centre for N.S.
Box 2128 East,
Dartmouth, N.S.
B2W 3Y2
(phone 434-6223)

Dalhousie University Archives
Halifax, N.S.
B3H 4H8
(phone 424-3615)

Federation of N.S. Heritage
Suite 305, 5515 Spring Garden Rd.
Halifax, N.S.
B3J 1G6
(phone 423-4677)

Genealogical Association of N.S.
Box 641, Station "M"
Halifax, N.S.
B3J 2T3

Maritime Command Museum
Admiralty House
CFB Halifax, N.S.
B3K 2X0
(phone 427-7740)

Milbrook Bank Council
Box 634
Truro, N.S.
B2N 5E5

Nova Scotia Museum
1747 Summer St.
Halifax, N.S.
B3H 3A6
(phone 429-4610)

Royal N.S. Historical Society
6016 University Ave.
Halifax, N.S.
B3H 1W4

REGIONAL

Beaton Institute
University College of Cape Breton
Box 5300
Sydney, N.S.
B1P 6L2
(phone 539-5300)

Cape Breton Genealogical Society
Box 53
Sydney, N.S.
B1P 6G4
(phone 562-4558)

Centre acadien de l'Université Ste-Anne
Church Point, N.S.
B0W 1M0
(phone 769-2114)

Eastern Counties Regional Library
Box 250
Mulgrave, N.S.
B0E 2G0
(phone 747-2597)

St. Francis Xavier University Library
Antigonish, N.S.
B2G 1C0
(phone 867-2267)

South Shore Genealogical Society
Box 901
Lunenburg, N.S.
B0J 2C0
(phone 634-8768)

COUNTY/MUNICIPAL

Admiral Digby Library
Box 938
Digby, N.S.
B0V 1A0
(phone 245-6322)

Annapolis Valley MacDonald Museum
Box 925
Middleton, N.S.
B0P 1X0
(phone 825-6116)

Cape Sable Historical Society
Barrington, N.S.
B0W 1E0

Chestico Museum
Box 144
Port Hood, N.S.
B0E 2W0
(phone 787-2617)

Colchester Historical Society Museum
29 Young St.
Truro, N.S.
B2N 5C5
(phone 895-8186)

Cumberland County Museum
150 Church St.
Amherst, N.S.
B4H 3C4
(phone 667-2561)

East Hants Historical Society
RR #1
Maitland, Hants Co.
Nova Scotia
B0N 1T0
(phone 261-2627)

Heritage Association of Antigonish
Box 1492
Antigonish, N.S.
B2G 2L7
(phone 863-4546)

Kings Historical Society
Ed Brownell
Berwick, N.S.
B0P 1E0
(phone 538-7221)

Musée Acadien
C.P. 98
Chéticamp, N.S.
B0E 1H0
(phone 224-2170)

North Cumberland Historical Society
R.R. #3
Pugwash, N.S.
B0K 1L0
(phone 243-2593)

North Shore Archives Society
Fraser Cultural Centre
Tatamagouche, N.S.
B0K 1V0

Old Courthouse Museum
Box 232
Guysborough, N.S.
B0H 1N0
(phone 533-4008)

Parkdale Maplewood Community Museum
R.R. #1
Barss Corner, N.S.
B0R 1A0
(phone 644-3288)

Pictou County Genealogical Society
Box 1210
Pictou, N.S.
B0K 1H0

Port Hastings Historical Society
Box 115
Port Hastings, N.S.
B0E 2T0
(phone 625-1295)

Queens County Museum
Box 1078
Liverpool, N.S.
B0T 1K0
(phone 354-4088)

Shelburne County Genealogical Society
Box 43
Shelburne, N.S.
B0T 1W0

Sunrise Trail Museum
R.R. #2
Tatamagouche, N.S.
B0K 1V0
(phone 657-2433)

West Hants Historical Society
140 Chestnut St.,
Windsor, N.S.
B0N 2T0
(phone 798-2958)

Yarmouth County Historical Society
Box 39
Yarmouth, N.S.
B5A 4B1
(phone 742-5539)

PERIODICALS

Cahiers de la Société historique acadienne, Box 2263, Station "A", Moncton, N.B. E1C 8J1.

Collections of the Royal Nova Scotia Historical Society, 6016 University Avenue, Halifax, N.S. B3H 1W4. Issued at irregular intervals since 1878 and now running to forty-two volumes, the *Collections* offer a mixture of material relating to the history of the province. Prices per book vary, but most are in the range of $7.50-$15.00.

The Nova Scotia Genealogist, published three times a year by the Genealogical Association of Nova Scotia, Box 641, Station "M", Halifax, N.S. B3J 2T3, $15.00 per year. Formerly issued (1971-1981) as the *Genealogical Newsletter*, this journal offers research articles, primary sources, book reviews, readers' queries, family bible data, etc.

The Nova Scotia Historical Review, published twice annually, $15.00 per year. The address is 6016 University Avenue, Halifax, N.S. B3H 1W4. Formerly issued (1971-1980) as the *Nova Scotia Historical Quarterly*, this magazine offers historical and genealogical articles with a high standard of editing.

SELECT BIBLIOGRAPHY

Beck, J. Murray. *The Government of Nova Scotia.* Toronto, 1957.

Bell, Winthrop P. *The "Foreign Protestants" and the Settlement of Nova Scotia.* Toronto, 1961.

Brebner, John Bartlett. *New England's Outpost: Acadia before the Conquest of Canada.* New York, 1927.

-----. *The Neutral Yankees of Nova Scotia; a marginal colony during the Revolutionary War.* Toronto, 1937.

Bumsted, J.J. *The People's Clearance: Highland Emigration to British North America 1770-1815.* Winnipeg, 1982.

Clark, Andrew Hill. *Acadia: The Geography of Early Nova Scotia to 1760.* Madison, 1968.

-----. "Old World Origins and Religious Adherence in Nova Scotia". *Geographical Review.* Vol. 50 (July 1960), pp. 317-344.

Conrad, Margaret, ed. *They Planted Well -- New England Planters in Maritime Canada.* Fredericton, N.B., 1988.

d'Entremont, Clarence J. *Histoire du Cap-Sable de l'an mil au traité de Paris, 1763.* Eunice, La., 1981.

Fergusson, C. Bruce. *Place-names and Places of Nova Scotia.* Halifax, 1967.

Gilroy, Marion. *Loyalists and Land Settlement in Nova Scotia.* Halifax, 1937.

The Loyalist Guide: Nova Scotia Loyalists and their documents. Halifax, 1984.

MacNutt, W.S. *The Atlantic Provinces: the Emergence of Colonial Society.* Toronto, 1967.

Marble, Allan E. *A Catalogue of Published Genealogies of Nova Scotia Families.* Halifax, 1979, 1984.

Martell, James S. *Immigration to and Emigration from Nova Scotia, 1815-1838.* Halifax, 1942.

Morris, Julie. *Tracing Your Ancestors in Nova Scotia.* Halifax, 1981, 1987.

Morrison, James H. *Common Heritage: An annotated bibliography of Ethnic groups in Nova Scotia.* Halifax, 1984.

Punch, Terrence M. *Genealogical Research in Nova Scotia.* Halifax, 1983.

-----. *In Which County? Nova Scotia Surnames from Birth Registers: 1864-1877.* Halifax, 1985.

----- and Cj Stevens. "Researching Nova Scotian Ancestry". *The New England Historical and Genealogical Register.* Vol. 138 (Oct. 1984), pp. 251-277.

Reid, John G. *Six Crucial Decades; Times of Change in the History of the Maritimes.* Halifax, 1987.

Tratt, Gertrude E.N. *A Survey and Listing of Nova Scotia Newspapers, 1752-1957.* Halifax, 1979.

Vaison, Robert. *Nova Scotia Past and Present: a bibliography and guide.* Halifax, 1976.

Wright, Esther Clark. *Planters and Pioneers, Nova Scotia, 1749-1775.* Hantsport, N.S., 1982.

PRINCE EDWARD ISLAND

by Orlo L. Jones, CG(C)

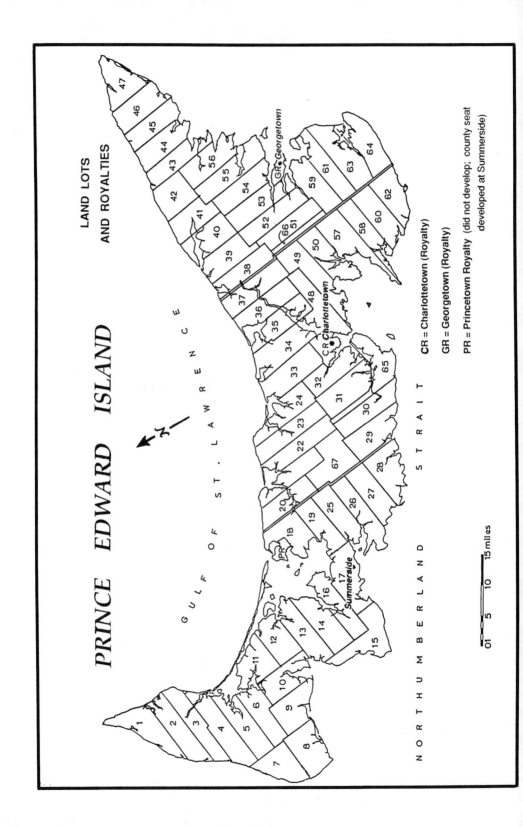

PRINCE EDWARD ISLAND

LAND LOTS AND ROYALTIES

N

GULF OF ST. LAWRENCE

NORTHUMBERLAND STRAIT

GR • Georgetown

CR Charlottetown

PR

Summerside

CR = Charlottetown (Royalty)

GR = Georgetown (Royalty)

PR = Princetown Royalty (did not develop; county seat
developed at Summerside)

01 5 10 15 miles

HISTORICAL OVERVIEW

Prince Edward Island was the last territory of what is now Atlantic Canada to be settled by Europeans. In 1720 the French established the first European settlement on the then-named Island of St. John, and held it until the deportation of the Acadians in 1758 by the British. A garrison of 200 troops left to hold the Island were the first British to live there. In 1763 the Island of St. John officially became a British territory when it was annexed to Nova Scotia.

To encourage settlement which would ensure that the Island remain British, the Government commissioned Surveyor Samuel Holland to survey and describe all of the land. Holland proceeded to divide it into three counties with a designated major town in each, and selected the harbour of Charlottetown to be the capital. He then subdivided the Island into 67 townships of approximately 20,000 acres each, and designated these numerically. In London in 1767 these townships were distributed by a lottery to persons "deserving Royal patronage"; since the land was allotted in this fashion the townships have been known as "Lots" with the township's numerical designation.

Two years later, in 1769, the Island of St. John was made a separate colony and was granted the right to form its own government and appoint its own officials - including the Rector of the Anglican Church, which was the established church of the colony. Settlement was slow: a few Acadians had escaped the deportation, and in 1770 a small number of prominent English and Irish military and government officials began arriving, as well as a few discharged soldiers and two small groups of Scottish immigrants. In 1772 the first Scottish Catholics landed, followed in 1775 by seven more Scottish families; however, it was 1784 before the first large number of immigrants came to establish a new homeland. This group, called United Empire Loyalists, consisted of 800 to 900 British soldiers, sympathizers, slaves, Hessians and others who had fled north after the American Revolution. An equal number of Scots were transported by Lord Selkirk in 1803, and this settlement began a trend whereby many from the British Isles left to look for their own land on this forested wilderness whose name was changed from the Island of St. John to Prince Edward Island in 1799.

It was 1873 before its status changed from a separate British colony to that of a province of the Dominion of Canada.

MAJOR REPOSITORIES

Prince Edward Island is small and compact, and most of its historical and gene-alogical records are housed in Charlottetown -- not in various communities of the province. The main record repositories in Charlottetown have worked together when collecting and indexing documents so that there is a minimum of duplica-tion, and all of these organizations are within a relatively comfortable walking distance. Because of this proximity, genealogical research on Prince Edward Is-land can be an enjoyable and exciting experience, facilitated by many finding aids.

1.   The starting point for Island research should be the Genealogical Depart-ment of the *Prince Edward Island Museum and Heritage Foundation*, estab-lished in 1970 to preserve and interpret the Island's past. In 1983 the P.E.I. Heritage Foundation became a decentralized museum system under its present name. One may become a member for $15.00 (individual) or $20.00 (family), which bestows free use of genealogical services, a subscription to *The Island Magazine*, and certain discounts. Copies of the microfilmed Master Name Index may be purchased through the Genealogical Depart-ment.

Directions: Entering Charlottetown from the west on University Avenue, turn right on Euston Street, then left on Rochford Street. Turn right on Kent Street. There is limited on-street parking, and a parking garage on Queen Street. The building is called "Beaconsfield". A small fee is charged to non-members of the organization or of the P.E.I. Genealogical Society. Visitors must sign the book upon entering the research room.

Facilities: One research room with limited seating and few staff; two mi-crofilm readers and one microfiche reader; limited photocopy-ing at 25¢ per copy; no interlibrary loan circulation. The few staff members cannot search printed genealogies or undertake extensive research. Mail or telephone service is limited to three specific queries when indexes will be checked. There is a small fee for this service, and a wait of six to twelve months is possible.

Holdings: Unique finding aids to save researchers countless hours. The MASTER NAME INDEX of over 500,000 cards is arranged al-phabetically. Names have been extracted from all Island gravestones prior to the 1970s, extant P.E.I. censuses, the 1881 and 1891 Canadian censuses of P.E.I., all known true pas-senger lists, marriage bonds and licenses (1814-46), inquest records (1787-1850), petitions (1770-1837), the Belfast Book of Records kept by Rev. A.M. Sinclair of his congregation in 1889, all names from *Hutchinson's P.E.I. Business Directory* of 1864, burial records made by Rev. T. Desbrisay in the *Royal Kalendar* 1805-23, newspapers (one per year of existing issues for 1791-1887 and certain selected years after this date), occupants of property from Meacham's 1880 Atlas, patrons list from the Atlas, St. Peter's Anglican Church (at Charlottetown) burial records from 1869-1961, most extant funeral home records, Penelope Cundall's birthday book, Benjamin Bremner's *Memories of Long Ago*, various store ledgers, a few school registers, earlier records of St. Paul's Anglican Church (Charlottetown), a number of Island community histories and some published genealogies of Island families, Richmond Parish Presbyterian church records (1821-46), etc.

Other holdings are the VITAL STATISTICS OF PRE-1886 BAPTISMS, compiled from existing church records; KINDEX, a cross-reference to those researching a given surname; COMPILED FAMILY FILES, published and manuscript genealogies, family abstracts and copies of documents given by researchers, the accuracy and documentation of which has not been checked; and a small INDEX OF BURIAL RECORD DATA. The genealogical service has a collection of community and church histories, P.E.I. history and reference books, genealogical guides and other publications such as journals and newsletters.

Publications:	The Museum publishes a few books on topics relating to the history of P.E.I. and sells a large variety of titles on Island subjects. It publishes *The Island Magazine* twice a year.
Address:	The Prince Edward Island Museum and Heritage Foundation, 2 Kent St., Charlottetown, P.E.I. C1A 1M6.
Telephone:	902-892-9127.
Hours:	Monday-Friday 9:00-12:00, 13:15-15:00, holidays excepted. Winter hours: Monday-Friday 10:00-12:00, 13:15-16:00, except holidays: Wednesday evenings 19:00-21:30 by appointment only. The Room is closed unless the Genealogist is present.

2.   *The Public Archives of Prince Edward Island* (P.A.P.E.I.), established in 1964 to acquire, preserve and conserve primary source material on the history of

P.E.I. The premises are open to the public, but one must sign the book upon entering. There are four microfilm readers, a small staff, and staff-operated photocopying and printout services are available for a small fee. A reference service is available by mail, while a ramp to the basement level enables the disabled to enter the premises.

Directions:	Entering Charlottetown from the west on University Avenue, turn right on Euston Street, go one block and turn left on Queen Street to Richmond Street. Turn left there and the building is on your left. P.A.P.E.I. is located on the fourth floor of the Hon. George Coles Bldg., a red brick structure.
Holdings:	Include early maps, land rental and lease records and conveyances for 1769-1900, a few school records, marriage licenses and bonds, census records, photographs, business records, private manuscripts, microfilmed church registers and government records. The last have been organized into record groups (R.G.), as follows:
R.G.1	papers of Lieutenant-Governors 1830-1872, Blue books, Colonial Secretary's correspondence, petitions and memorials, etc.
R.G.5	Executive Council minutes 1770-1955, petitions 1780-1915, warrants of survey, licenses of occupation 1809-38, confederation documents, etc.
R.G.6	Supreme Court Records (restricted -- written permission of the prothonotary is required for their use).
R.G.7	Colonial & Provincial Secretary, letter books 1840-96, license ledgers 1825-74, etc.
R.G.8	Provincial Treasurer and Dept. of Finance, warrant books 1812-91.
R.G.9	Records of the Collector of Customs, ship registrations, records of shipping inwards and outwards, etc.
R.G.10	Records of the Board and Dept. of Education, includes teacher lists 1871-77, teachers' licences 1879-96, registers of teachers' salaries 1870-1919, school visitors' annual reports 1837-1940.

R.G.14   United Empire Loyalist allotments and papers.

R.G.15   Records of the Commissioner of Crown and Public
                Lands, including valuation books for 1777-1895, lease
                agreements between Edward Cunard and others,
                Crown Land deeds from 1792, rent books, petitions, etc.

R.G.19   Vital statistics kept by district registrars' offices from ca.
                1906-1912, some school records, teachers' registers, class
                books, etc., incomplete.

R.G.20   Records of the City of Charlottetown: poll books 1863-
                84 are incomplete etc.

Other parts of the R.G. series are more recent and of less interest to genealogists as a rule.

Address: The Public Archives of Prince Edward Island
                Box 1000
                Charlottetown, P.E.I.
                C1A 7M4

Telephone: 902-368-4290

Hours: Monday-Friday 8:00-16:00 in summer,
                Monday-Friday 8:30-17:00 in winter.

VITAL RECORDS

The official registration of births, deaths, and marriages for P.E.I. was not com-
pulsory until 1906, when it was undertaken by the Division of Vital Statistics.
Records for the earlier years are incomplete. Prior to 1905 the Division made an
index to baptisms recorded in church registers, and they hold this index for the
years 1886-1905. This information is considered confidential and privileged, so
these records are closed to researchers. Upon receipt of the name of a person, the
date and place of the event and the names of spouses or parents and your relationship to the person, a staff member will check the records for you. A three-year
search including issue of a regular or short-form certificate, if the record is found,
costs $5.00. The cost of searches and long-form certificates (only for visa, social
services or genealogical requirements) is $10.00 a name.

Except for the long-form birth certificates and marriage records the Island's certificates give very little information. Service by mail may entail a slight waiting period. Information typically given on the certificates is the following:

A regular *birth certificate* states only the full name, date and place of birth, and sex. The long form adds the names and birthplaces of the parents.

A short form *marriage certificate* gives the names, date and place of marriage and the birthplaces of bride and groom only. The certified copy of the original marriage registration is more informative, but restricted, so you must state why you need a certified copy.

A P.E.I. *death certificate* gives name, date and place of death, age, sex, marital status and place of regular residence only; no parents' or spouses' names are given.

The department of Health and Social Services had no means of verifying for pension purposes the ages of those born before 1906, so they arranged with the Island churches to make an index from all existing baptismal records kept by the churches. The pre-1886 part of this index is in the Genealogical Dept. of the P.E.I. Museum and Heritage Foundation and is open to the public; P.A.P.E.I. has a microfilm copy. The baptismal index 1886-1905 is held by Vital Statistics and is not open to researchers.

In 1832 a law provided that all appointed clergy could legally perform marriages. If banns were not read in church it was required that a couple obtain a license, and after 1833 a marriage bond was demanded of both parties before a license could be obtained. The bonds guaranteed there was no known lawful impediment to a legal marriage. These *Marriage Bonds and Licenses* are held by the P.A.P.E.I. and have been indexed by both brides' and grooms' names; the bonds cover the period 1849-1902, and the licenses 1787-1901, with some for 1904-1906.

Marriage certificates also exist for 1906, and from 1916-1920. After 1832 records of applications for marriage licenses and the registration of marriages were supposed to be submitted to the Surrogate's office within six months of the event. Sixteen of these Surrogate's marriage books have survived: 1797-1831 for licenses only, 1832-1932 for licenses and registrations. The P.A.P.E.I. has all sixteen books on microfilm. A project is underway by the P.E.I. Genealogical Society to index the post-1832 records by both brides' and grooms' names. This index is being incorporated into the genealogical holdings of the P.E.I. Museum and Heritage Foundation.

The P.A.P.E.I. also holds a microfilm copy of the applications for marriage licenses issued by the Deputy Prothonotary of Prince County for 26 Dec. 1879-23 Dec. 1940 and for 27 Jan. 1941-29 Sept. 1969, as well as those issued by the Deputy Prothonotary of Kings County for 1 July 1879-9 Feb. 1970.

A number of very fragile books exist at the P.A.P.E.I., described in accessioning simply as "Records of Births, Queens Co. c1906-c1912, and record of Deaths, Kings County, c1906-c1912", as well as similar records for all three counties. No source is stated. These records were kept in districts very like or the same as our townships or Lots. Those death records exist for many but not all of the districts.

Adoption records on P.E.I. are closed. Those after the 1930s are held by the Division of Vital Statistics and are kept legally sealed. If you feel these records should be opened you may apply for a court order, but it is stated to be almost impossible to gain access to these records. Before 1916 adoptions were undertaken informally, so if the birth surname, birthdate, etc. are known, it may be possible to obtain the names of parents.

Directions:	Entering Charlottetown from the west on University Avenue, turn right on Euston Street. Turn left on Rochford Street and follow it to Haviland Street. The office is located in the W.J.P. MacMillan Bldg. on the corner to your right. There is limited on-street parking.
Address:	Prince Edward Island Division of Vital Statistics Box 2000 Charlottetown, P.E.I. C1A 7N8
Telephone:	902-368-4420, extension 215
Hours:	Monday-Friday 8:00-16:00 in summer Monday-Friday, 8:30-17:00 in winter.

CENSUS RECORDS

A number of early French census returns were made for the Island. Those for 1728, 1734, 1735 and LaRoque's in 1752 have been carded and are held by the P.E.I. Museum and Heritage Foundation. The first British census was taken in 1798 but the original does not exist; however, a copy was published in Duncan Campbell's *History of Prince Edward Island*. There is no other surviving census until 1841, and the census of that year lacks twenty-five of the sixty-seven lots. A census survives

for Charlottetown, Royalty, and Lot thirty-one dated 1848; the 1861 census survives for sixty-one lots; and the 1871 census survives only for lots thirty-four and
thirty-six. These English returns give only the names of the heads of household
and a breakdown by age and sex of household members; the originals of these are
kept by the P.A.P.E.I., but the public must use microfilmed copies at Confederation Centre Library or Robertson Library of the University of P.E.I.

The only Canadian census returns for P.E.I. which are open to the public (1881
and 1891) give names and approximate ages of all persons, as well as other data.
The 1891 census is missing for lots twenty-one and twenty-two. Census returns to
1891 have been carded. The cards are held by the P.E.I. Museum and Heritage
Foundation. Microfilm copies of these census reports may be borrowed from the
National Archives of Canada on interlibrary loan.

LAND RECORDS

Land records are the most complex body of Island records used by genealogists. All of those before 1900 are kept by the P.A.P.E.I. and may be divided into
the following types:

1) *Grants* or gifts of land by the Crown or Government were the means by
   which the first Island landowners procured land in 1767. These landowners seldom lived in the province and usually rented their land to
   tenants. Land transactions taking place while P.E.I. was a territory of
   Nova Scotia may be sought in records at the P.A.N.S. After 1769 they
   should be located in the P.A.P.E.I.

2) *Rent Books* or ledgers kept by landowners showing their tenants' records of
   payments have survived for forty-four lots over varying times.

3) *Lease Books* show transactions between proprietors and the first tenant. All
   subsequent leases were recorded on this original lease. To determine
   who held the first leases one has to use old cadastral maps located at
   the P.A.P.E.I.

4) *Freehold Conveyances* for the whole Island have been indexed separately by
   grantors and grantees. Prior to 1873 conveyances for all three counties
   were kept in one set of books, but between 1873 and 1900 those for
   each county are kept separately.

5) *Mortgage Books* for 1873-1900, but these are of little help to genealogists.

6) *Government's Conveyances or Township Ledgers.* Many of the original proprietors either refused to sell to tenants or charged exorbitant prices. After

the Land Purchase Acts of 1853 and 1875 the government forced absentee landowners to sell their land to the government, which gave tenants first option to buy at a fixed and reasonable term. These records are indexed.

7) *Post-1900 Land Records* (conveyances and mortgages) are kept in the Land Registry Office -- originals for Queens and Kings counties, microfilms for Prince County. These records have been indexed by the first and third letters of the surnames.

Address: The Land Registry Office
             P.O. Box 2000, Jones Bldg.
             Kent Street
             Charlottetown, P.E.I.
             C1A 7N8

Telephone: 902-368-4591

The office is located on Kent Street between West and Rochford streets, and keeps regular civil service hours Monday to Friday. There is limited on-street parking, and a very small staff and space to help genealogical researchers.

PROBATE RECORDS

Probate records are indexed and kept in the Estates Division of the Supreme Court. Those names beginning with Mac or Mc are not filed under M but under the first letter of the last part of the surname. (e.g., MacKinnon is to be found under letter K). The earliest recorded will was registered in 1807, although unrecorded wills extend to the late 1700s. It is believed that earlier wills were probated in an English ecclesiastical court.

After 1807 all wills for the province were registered in Charlottetown, and letters of administration for the estates of persons who died intestate are here as well. Wills and letters of administration were recorded separately until 1901 when they were combined. Both the indexes to wills and administrations and copies of the wills are available to the public. Specific estate files of original documents may be brought from the vault upon request.

Directions: Proceed down Rochford Street/Haviland to Water Street, turn left on Water Street. The office is located in Sir Louis Henry Davies Law Court Bldg., 42 Water Street. Limited on-street parking. Photocopying available.

Address:	Estates Division of the Supreme Court
	Box 205
	Charlottetown, P.E.I.
	C1A 7K4
Telephone:	902-892-9131
Hours:	Monday-Friday 8:00-16:00 in summer,
	Monday-Friday 8:30-17:00 in winter.

NEWSPAPERS

Island newspapers did not survive until 1791, when the *Royal Gazette and Miscellany*, filled with world news but little local news, was published. Rarely did birth, marriage and death information appear unless the person was prominent or from Charlottetown. The *P.E.I. Register* with Island news in general began in 1823. However, obituaries as we know them seldom appeared before the end of the nineteenth century and often not then. Many issues of early newspapers are missing.

Most Island newspapers are available on microfilm at Confederation Centre Library or Robertson Library of the University of P.E.I. They may be borrowed on interlibrary loan from the National Library, Ottawa, as well.

CHURCH RECORDS

Church records are invaluable for the period before civil registration began in 1906. These records vary by denomination and even within denominations. For a number of years after 1777 the Church of England was the only established church on the Island and therefore has the oldest records kept under the English regime. Generally speaking, other denominations were served only by visiting missionaries and clergy and their records, except for some early Catholic baptisms kept by Acadian churches and a few items at St. Andrew's Roman Catholic church in Mount Stewart for 1809-1810, have not surfaced. Most Catholic records are missing prior to 1829 (while the Island was under the diocese of Québec). Those after 1890 are restricted. Most Protestant churches which performed adult baptisms did not keep records of them.

Usual church records are those of baptism, marriage, death and confirmation. Such records for most Island churches have been microfilmed and are held by the P.A.P.E.I., but each church has established its own policy as to the accessibility of these records to the public. Frequently records are missing over a considerable period of time. A guide to those church records available to the public as of 23 October 1986 is as follows (**A** Anglican; **B** Baptist; **C** Catholic; **ChCh** Church of Christ; **CS** Church of Scotland; **M** Methodist; **P** Presbyterian; **U** United):

PLACE	(Denomination)	BAPTISMS	MARRIAGES	DEATHS	BURIALS
Alberton	A	1859-1973	1859-1973		1859-1973
	C	1879-1890	1879-1890		1879-1890
	M/U	1867-1954	1867-1954		1867-1954
	P	1865-1867	1855-1866		1865-1867
		1891-1954	1891-1910		1891-1936
Bedeque	U	1821-1952	1828-1976		1918-1975
Bedeque North	U	1826-1985	1883-1984	1975-1985	1888-1985
Belfast	P	1823-1849			
		1853-1977			
Belle River	CS	1868-1894	1944-1967		
Bideford	U	1875-1946	1875-1882		1906-1970
			1906-1970		
Birch Hill	CS	1878-1900			
Bloomfield	C	1839-1890	1839-1890		1839-1890
Bonshaw/Tryon	P	1867-1891	1899-1925		
		1894-1921			
Bonshaw/Hampton					
Victoria	U	1920-1968	1920-1968	1920-1968	
Brae	C	1833-1890	1933-1890	1833-1890	
Breadalbane	ChCh	1897-1956			
	P	1845-1905	1852-1862		
	U	1926-1971	1926-1971	1926-1971	
Bridgetown	M/P	1897-1905			
Brookfield	CS	1868-1894			
	P	1918-1948	1918-1948	1918-1935	
Burlington	A*	1833-1947	1823-1947		1842-1947
Caledonia	P	1888-1927	1890-1921	1890-1921	
			1925		
Canoe Cove	CS	1853-1900			
Cape Traverse	CS	1853-1900			
Cardigan	C	1868-1890	1868-1890		1868-1890
Cardigan Bridge	C	1874-1890	1875-1890	1879-1890	
Cascumpec	C	1839-1868	1860-1868		
	P		1832-1854		
			1867-1890		
			1899-1900		

Cavendish	P	1878-c1925	1877-1906	1897,1904- 1905,1927- 1928	
	U	c1925-1964	1924-1964	1924-1964	
Charlottetown					
St. Dunstan's	C	1820,1830- 1890	1830-1876		1858-1876
Christian Ch.			1897-1954		
St. Paul's	A	1777-1939	1780-1819 1827-1939		1827-1947
St. Peter's	A*	1869-1982	1870-1981		1961-1982
First Baptist		1837-1955		1874-1931	
St. James	P	1849-1974	1887-1891 1930-1975		1930-1961 1963-1975
Trinity	U	1836-1934	1836-1980		1836-1980
Cherry Valley					
(Bible Ch)		1848-1913	1884-1913	1888-1913	
Churchill	CS	1894-1928			
Clyde River	P	1887-1922	1860-1873 1895-1926	1890-1982	
Cornwall	C	1887-1890	1887-1890		1887-1890
	M/U	1857-1966	1857-1876 1880-1901 1904-1965	1890-1966	1867-1870
	P	1887-1922	1860-1873 1895-1926	1890-1932	
Covehead	C	1887-1890	1887-1890	1887-1890	
Crapaud	A*	1843-1951	1843-1952		1845-1952
Cross Roads					
(Scotch Baptist)		1810-1896	1843-1874		1816-1844
DeSable	CS	1858-1900			
Dundas	M/P	1897-1905			
East Point	B		1919-1980	1920-1980	
	C	1835-1890	1853-1872		1853-1872
Egmont Bay	C	1821-1890	1821-1890		1821-1890
Ellerslie	A*	1842,1846- 1911 1914-1950	1842,1846- 1950		1847-1950
(Port Hill Parish)					
Elmsdale	P/U	1895-1954	1895-1954		1895-1954
Fairfield	C	1835-1890	1853-1872	1880-1890	1853-1872 1880-1890
Fort Augustus	C	1854-1890	1854-1890	1854-1890	
French River (New London Parish)	A*	1833-1947	1833-1947		1842-1947
Georgetown	A*	1842-1895	1842-1895		1855-1895

Georgetown	A*				1947,1959 1965
	C	1855-1890	1875-1890	1875-1890	
	M/U	1854-1961	1881-1963	1838-1963	
Glasgow Road	CS	1894-1928			
Grand River	C	1842-1890	1842-1890		1842-1890
Granville	P	1893-1914	1893-1913	1894-1915	
Guernsey Cove (Bible Ch)		1842-1914	1878-1915		
	M	1792-1841 1869-1879			
Hartsville	P	1845-1875 1884-1908	1852-1862		
Highfield	CS	1894-1928			
Hopefield	P	1892-1925	1915-1969		1915-1953
Hope River	C	1881-1890	1881-1890		
Hunter River	P	1918-1947	1918-1948	1918-1935	
	U	1880-1976	1916-1984	1914-1976	
Indian River	C	1838-1890	1838-1890		1838-1890
Iona	C	1865-1890	1874-1890	1865-1890	
Kelly's Cross	C	1851-1890	1851-1890		
Kensington	A*	1833-1947	1833-1947		1842-1947
	U	1917-1986	1917-1986	1917-1986	
Kinkora	C	1860-1890	1860-1890		1860-1890
Lennox Island	C	1833-1890	1842-1890	1879-1890	
Little Pond	C	1865-1890	1865-1890		1865-1890
Little Sands	P	1892-1955	1915-1969		1915-1953
	U	1956-1969	1933-1943		1958-1969
Little York	M	1857-1875, 1880 1886-1966	1857-1876 1882-1901 1904-1965	1908-1966	1867-1870
Lot 7 St. Mark's	C	1868-1890	1868-1890		1868-1890
Lot 11	A*	1842, 1846-1911 1914-1950	1842, 1846-1950		1847-1950
	C	1876-1890	1976-1890		1876-1890
Lot 48 Mermaid	CS	1893-1928	1921-1926	1925-1926	
Lot 55 - St. George's	C	1836-1890			
Lot 65 - St. Anne's	C	1861-1890	1861-1890		
Lower Montague	U	1965-1981	1965-1982	1965-1982	
Malpeque	C	1817-1835	1817-1835	1817-1835	

Margate	U	1886-1968	1886-1965	1893-1967	
		(Early marriage and birth records 1778-1843)			
Marshfield	P	1862-1978	1866-1973	1877-1962, 1977	
Miscouche	C	1817-1887	1817-1835		1835-1887
Montague	B		1841-1842	1832-1924	
	C	1872-1890			
	ChCh	1967-1978	1953-1978	1926-1939 1968-1978	
	U	1877-1981	1881-1982	1884-1982	
Montrose	P/U	1895-1954	1895-1954		1895-1954
Morell	C	1881-1890			
Mt. Stewart	C	1809-1810 1835-1890	1838-1890		1856-1890
	U	1871-1961	1877-1912 1915-1917 1919-1962	1871-1961	
Murray Harbour (Bible Ch)		1842-1915	1878-1915		
	ChCh	1899-1974			
	M	1792-1841 1869-1879			
	P	1892-1955	1915-1969		1915-1953
	U	1956-1969	1933-1943		1958-1969
Murray River (Bible Ch)		1842-1914	1878-1915	1878-1915	
	CS	1878-1900			
	P	1892-1955	1915-1969		1915-1953
	U	1864-1969	1933-1943		1958-1969
New London - see French River					
Orwell Head	CS	1853-1899			
	P	c1886-1925	c1887-1925	c1887-1925	
	U	c1925-1966	c1925-1967	c1925-1965	
Palmer Road	C*	1878-1890	1878-1890		1878-1890
Port Hill	A*	1842, 1846-1911 1914-1973	1864-1973		1847-1973
Port La Joye	C	1749-1758	1749-1758	1749-1758	
Pownal	M/U	1856-1964	1856-1967	1891-1964	
Princetown	U	1860-1967	1860-1966	1904-1967	
Richmond Bay East	P	1885-1967	1894-1968		1898-1968

Richmond Bay West	P	1885-1980	1932-1981	1907-1910 1931-1982	
Richmond Bay	U	1885-1967	1894-1968		1898-1968
Richmond Parish	A	1821, 1823-1866	1824-1864		1824-1864
	P	1820-1847	1821-1834		
Rollo Bay	C	1847-1890	1847-1890		1878-1890
Rustico	C	1812-1890	1812-1890		1812-1890
Seven Mile Bay	C	1846-1890	1846-1900		
St. Eleanors	A*	1821, 1823-1957	1824-1957		1824-1864 1872-1945
St. George's Parish	A*	1842-1895	1842-1895		1855-1895 1947,1959 1965
St. Margarets	C*	1881-1890	1881-1890	1881-1890	
St. Peters	C	1849-1890	1885-1890		1885-1890
St. Pierre du Nord	C	1721-1758	1721-1758	1721-1758	
Souris	A*	1894-1917 1931,1935 1956,1960	1899,1903 1912,1916 1976		1899-1916 1931-1932 1963
	C	1864-1890	1864-1890		1864-1890
	U	1862-1985	1873-1881 1890-1891 1894, 1899-1985	1870-1985	
Springfield	A*	1850-1971	1857-1928 1950-1956 1972,1974		1848-1979
Strathalbyn	P	1845-1875 1884-1908	1852-1862		
Sturgeon	C	1867-1890	1867-1890		1867-1890
	M/U	1792-1841 1869-1879 1965-1981	1965-1982	1965-1982	
Summerside	A*	1821, 1823-1957	1824-1957		1824-1864 1872-1945
	C	1821, 1823-1957	1824-1957		1824-1864 1872-1945
	ChCh	1858-1962	1893-1960	1892-1962	
	U	1866-1960	1868-1885 1889-1893		1916-1965

Summerside	U		1916-1964		
Three Rivers	B	1836-1890	1841-1842	1832-1924	
	C	1836-1890			
	M	1792-1841			
		1869-1879			
Tignish	C	1831-1890	1831-1890		1831-1854
					1878-1879
Tracadie	C	1845-1890	1861-1890		1887-1890
Tryon	M/U	1876-1968	1876-1968	1908-1910	
				1918-1968	
Valleyfield	U		1848-1982	1863-1982	
Vernon River					
(Bible Ch)		1848-1913	1884-1913	1888-1913	
	C	1838-1890	1845-1846		1868-1890
			1855-1860		
			1868-1890		
	U	1809-1810	c1838-1967	1912-1968	
		1835-1967			
Wellington	C	1884-1890			1884-1890
West River	P	1887-1922	1860-1873	1890-1932	
			1895-1926		
White Sands					
(Bible Ch/					
M/U)		1792-1915	1878-1915		

Twenty Anglican or Roman Catholic churches possess confirmation records, the earliest dating from 1864. Such churches are indicated by an asterisk (*). Specific birth records exist for a few churches as follows:

Bonshaw United 1917-1919
Clyde River Pres. 1908-1926
Cornwall Methodist 1908-1926
Cornwall Presbyterian 1908-1926
East Point Baptist 1941-1980 (Birth book 1871-1962)
Little York Methodist/United 1920-1926
Lot 48 Church of Scotland 1856-1928
Richmond Bay East Presbyterian 1919-1964
Richmond Bay West Presbyterian 1907-1911
Richmond Bay United 1919-1964
Valleyfield United 1822-1981
West River Presbyterian 1908-1926

CEMETERY RECORDS

All pre-1970 gravestones in Island cemeteries and private graveyards have been transcribed and carded by surname and lot, and are incorporated into the Master Name Index of the P.E.I. Museum and Heritage Foundation. Generally all information on the stone was recorded on the card and cross references were compiled for all surnames on the stones. Many of the earliest grave markers have been lost due to erosion and breakage, while some people did not erect stones. P.A.P.E.I. holds a microfilm copy of these cemetery transcriptions. Transcriptions of individual cemeteries may be purchased from the P.E.I. Genealogical Society.

IMMIGRATION RECORDS

Immigration records are scanty since passenger lists were not required until the British Passenger Act was passed in 1855. A few very earlier lists have survived, have been published in the *The Island Magazine*, and have been indexed and added to the Master Name Index. Existing issues of one newspaper per year, and custom house records for 1790-1809 and 1819-1827, have been checked for the names of passengers who apparently travelled first class; the results have been indexed and published in *The Island Magazine*. These records are incomplete, however, because they did not record names of passengers in steerage, and many issues of the earlier newspapers and custom house records are missing.

At first rather few boats came into Charlottetown to clear customs. Instead captains beached their vessels on the sandy shores and passengers waded ashore at low tide; custom house reports have no record of these persons. It is said that ages of children given on passenger lists may have been exaggerated, sometimes as a means of getting a cheaper passage if the child was rather small for its age, or even made older to get a larger allowance of food and water.

SOCIETIES AND LIBRARIES

Most smaller institutions in areas other than Charlottetown have copies of some of the material found in the major repositories. These institutions may be more accessible for people visiting other parts of the Island. The list below is arranged alphabetically by the name of the area where each institution is located.

SOCIETIES:

1) *Alberton Museum*, Church St., Alberton, P.E.I. COB 1B0

Contact:	Dr. Allan MacRae, CG(C)
Location:	Old courthouse on Church St., Alberton
Open:	Mid-June to the end of August
Holdings:	Probably the largest collection outside Charlottetown of materials on families from the west Prince County area. There are facilities for genealogical research.

2) *Centre de Récherches Acadiennes*, Musée Acadien, Box 159, Miscouche, P.E.I. COB 1T0

Contact:	Cécile Gallant
Location:	Route 2 west of Summerside, on the right as one enters the village of Miscouche.
Telephone:	902-436-6237
Open:	22 June-12 September, 9:00-17:00
Holdings:	Books, church records, newspapers, family bibles and personal papers on P.E.I. Acadians for the period 1721-1890.
Facilities:	Will answer genealogical enquiries by mail or telephone, or make materials available year round by appointment only. There is limited staff to assist in genealogical research.

3) *O'Leary Library and Museum Association*, O'Leary, P.E.I. COB 1V0.

Contact:	Irma Sweet
Location:	P.E.I. Potato Museum in O'Leary.
Open:	Mid June to end of August, 10:00-16:00.
Holdings:	"Books with some family histories and personal papers for the 1850-1986 period in the O'Leary District."
Facilities:	Limited amount of genealogically useful materials, but will endeavour to answer enquiries by mail.

4) *Farmer's Bank Museum*, South Rustico, Hunter River R.R. #3, P.E.I. C0A 1N0.

Contact:	Arthur Buote, President
Location:	On route 243 next to St. Augustine's Church
Open:	July and August 10:00-1700. Closed the rest of the year.

Holdings: Census, church and cemetery records, and some school records dating from 1812 to the present for North Rustico, South Rustico, Hope River and Hunter River areas are available for researchers to use in person. There is no staff to answer postal or telephone enquiries.

5) *Eptek National Exhibition Centre*, Box 1378, Summerside, P.E.I. C1N 1A9.

Contact: Nonie Fraser, Director
Location: Summerside Waterfront Mall, Water St. East
Open: Monday closed
     Tuesday, Wednesday, Friday, 8:30-17:00
     Thursday 8:30-21:00
     Saturday 10:00-17:00
     Sunday 13:00-17:00
Holdings: Census and church records, books, newspapers for Prince County for 1865-1951. There is one microfilm reader, but no staff to aid researchers or to answer postal or telephone enquiries.

6) *Dalton Centre Inc.*, Tignish, P.E.I. C0B 2B0

Contact: J. Henri Gaudet, President
Holdings: Mr. Gaudet will answer postal queries or make his personal history files available by appointment when he is home. These files consist of census, church and cemetery records, old newspapers, personal papers, *L'Impartial Illustré* and copies of research papers by others about the Acadians and people of the Tignish area from 1799 to the present.

LIBRARIES:

1) *Confederation Centre Public Library*, Box 7000,
Charlottetown, P.E.I. C1A 8G8.

Contact: Alison Ann Heckbert
Location: At corner of Richmond and Queen streets in Charlottetown.
Open: *Winter Hours*
     Monday closed
     Tuesday to Thursday 10:00-21:00
     Friday & Saturday 10:00-17:00
     Sunday 13:00-17:00

Summer Hours
Monday-Thursday 10:00-21:00
Friday 10:00-17:00
Saturday & Sunday closed

Facilities: Staff must concentrate on traditional duties so that little help with genealogical research should be expected. There are finding aids, a card catalogue and a newspaper index. There are open stacks and no fees. Outside there is limited on-street parking.

Holdings: The usual holdings of public libraries, but for those preparing community histories or interested in Island history and genealogy the Prince Edward Island Collection is of particular interest. It includes over 600 items related directly to P.E.I. or works written by or about Islanders. The pamphlet collection contains over 600 items covering the same subject area. Some of this material is unique and may not leave the library, but there are copies of many titles which may be borrowed. Island newspapers on microfilm, census records dating from 1841, books, journals, business directories and almanacs are available here.

2) *Robertson Library*, U.P.E.I., Charlottetown, P.E.I. C1A 4P3. Located on university campus to the left as one enters the city on Trans Canada Highway 1 from the west. Hours of opening vary by season. Visitors should check with the Library in advance.

Facilities: No fees, on-campus parking, but the staff's primary responsibility is to members of the university, whose needs must be given priority.

Holdings: Open stacks; the 1841, 1861 and 1881 census returns, and extensive holdings of microfilmed newspapers. Filby's *Passenger and Immigration Lists Bibliography* and the index to *Passenger and Immigration Lists* are available at the Information Desk. The general collections include some "how to" books, a few printed genealogies, and newsletters from the United Empire Loyalist Association and the P.E.I. Genealogical Society.

PRINCE EDWARD ISLAND GENEALOGICAL SOCIETY:

The Society was formed in 1976 to supplement the work of the P.E.I. Heritage Foundation and as a forum to exchange hints, information and methodology among members. Membership entitles one to free use of the genealogical services of the P.E.I. Museum and Heritage Foundation. There are four public meetings and four newsletters a year but no separate holdings nor staff to undertake research. The Society also offers individual P.E.I. cemetery transcriptions for sale. The address is Box 2744, Charlottetown, P.E.I. C1A 8C4. Individual membership is $6.00 a year, and family and overseas memberships are $8.00 a year.

PERIODICALS

1) *The Island Magazine,* published twice a year by the P.E.I. Museum and Heritage Foundation, 2 Kent St., Charlottetown, P.E.I. C1A 1M6, for $7.00 per year, included in the membership package of the Museum. The first issue is dated Fall-Winter 1976; back issues are available from the editor, Dr. Edward MacDonald.

2) *The Abegweit Review,* published twice a year. "Editorial policy stipulates that at least eighty percent of the material published...must be Island-oriented." The editor is W.P. MacIntyre. Subscriptions are $13.00 per year, from U.P.E.I., Charlottetown, P.E.I. C1A 4P3.

BIBLIOGRAPHY

Arsenault, Georges. *Histoire de l'émigration chez les Acadiens de L'île-du-Prince-Edouard.* Summerside, 1980.

-----. *Initiation à l'histoire acadienne.* Summerside, 1984.

-----. *La religion et les Acadiens à l'île-du-Prince-Edouard, 1720-1980.* Summerside, 1983.

Babineau, René. *A Brief History of Acadia 1604-1984, or Résumé d'histoire d'Acadie 1604-1984.*

Baglole, Harry. *Exploring Island History.* Charlottetown, 1977.

Blanchard, Henri. *Histoire des Acadiens de l'île-du-Prince-Edouard.* Summerside, 1956.

-----. *The Acadians of Prince Edward Island 1720-1964.* Ottawa, 1964.

-----. *Rustico, une paroisse acadienne de l'île-du-Prince-Edouard.* 1937, 1979.

Bolger, F.W.P. *Canada's Smallest Province.* Charlottetown, 1973.

Bumsted, J.M. *The People's Clearance 1770-1815.* Edinburgh, 1982.

Callbeck, Lorne C. *My Island, My People.* Charlottetown, 1979.

-----. *The Cradle of Confederation.* Fredericton, N.B., 1964.

Campbell, D. *History of Prince Edward Island.* Charlottetown, 1875.

Clark, Andrew H. *Three Centuries and the Island.* Toronto, 1959.

Greenhill, Basil, and Gifford, Ann. *Westcountrymen in Prince Edward's Isle.* Toronto, 1967.

Harvey, Daniel C. *The French Régime in Prince Edward Island.* New Haven, 1926. There was a reprint by Ams Press, New York, 1970.

-----. ed. *Journeys to the Island of St. John.* Toronto, 1955.

Hennessey, M.F., ed. *The Catholic Church in Prince Edward Island 1720-1979.* Charlottetown, 1979.

Jones, Orlo, and Haslam, Doris, eds., *An Island Refuge: Loyalists and Disbanded Troops on the Island of Saint John.* Summerside, 1983.

Jones, Orlo. *Family History in Prince Edward Island, A Genealogical Research Guide.* Charlottetown, 1981.

MacMillan, John C. *The Catholic Church in P.E.I. from 1835 to 1891.* Québec, 1913.

MacQueen, Malcolm A. *Hebridean Pioneers.* Winnipeg, 1957.

-----. *Skye Pioneers and "The Island".* Winnipeg, 1929.

Meacham, J.H. *Illustrated Historical Atlas of Prince Edward Island.* 1880, reprinted by Mika, Belleville, 1977.

O'Grady, Brendan, ed. *The Abegweit Review.* (The issues of Spring 1983 and Winter 1985 devoted to the Irish on the Island.)

Pollard, James B. *Historical Sketch of the Eastern Regions of New France, also P.E.I., Military and Civil.* Charlottetown, 1898.

Rankin, Robert A. *Down at the Shore: A History of Summerside, Prince Edward Island.* Charlottetown, 1890.

Rayburn, Alan. *Geographical Names of Prince Edward Island.* Ottawa, 1973.

Rogers, Irene L. *Charlottetown, the Life in its Buildings.* Charlottetown, 1983.

Sinnott, F.H. *History of the Baptists of Prince Edward Island.* 1973.

Stewart, John. *An Account of Prince Edward Island in the Gulph of St. Lawrence.* London, 1806, reprinted 1967.

Warburton, Alexander B. *A History of Prince Edward Island.* Saint John, 1923.

Warburton, A.B., and MacKinnon, Donald. *Past and Present of P.E.I.* Charlottetown, c. 1906.

Weale, David, and Baglole, Harry. *The Island and Confederation, The End of an Era.* Charlottetown, 1973.

REGIONAL BODIES

by Stephen A. White CG(C)

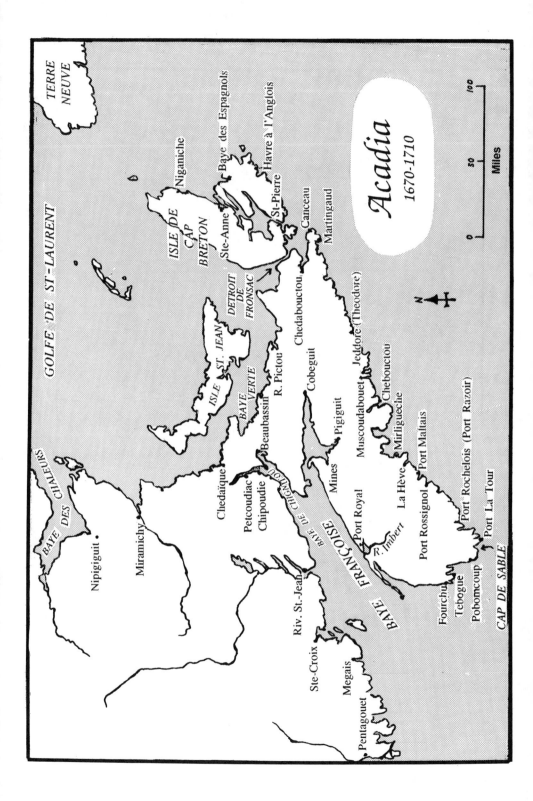

Acadia
1670-1710

REGIONAL BODIES

Genealogical Institute of the Maritimes

1. *Background*

The Genealogical Institute of the Maritimes is a non-profit corporation chartered by the federal government of Canada in 1983. Its main purpose is to qualify genealogists, and in the process advance genealogical professionalism, set standards of practice, provide impartial screening of applicants by other members of the genealogical community, and distribute lists of qualified professionals and other useful information. The work of the Institute has been encouraged and endorsed by the Council of Maritime Premiers.

2. *Constitution*

The Institute is run by a Board of Governors who meet semi-annually. Members of the Board include, *ex officio*, the provincial archivists, the presidents of the genealogical societies of each of the constituent provinces, and the director of the Centre d'Etudes acadiennes, or their delegates, and two well-known genealogists from each province who serve as judges and examiners of candidates. The Board elects, from among its members, a president, vice-president, treasurer, and recording and corresponding secretaries. The corresponding secretary also acts as registrar, maintaining the records of the Institute.

3. *Categories of Certification and Membership*

The Institute examines and certifies persons who desire to establish their competence in genealogical research. The Institute issues two types of certificate: Certified Genealogist (Canada) (CG(C)) and Genealogical Record Searcher (Canada) (GRS(C)). Each demands skill in the use of records, the ability to prepare proper reports of findings, and ethical conduct.

The GRS(C) must have a working knowledge of genealogical principles; he or she must know, understand, and be able to work comfortably with genealogical records -- manuscript, typescript, or printed -- and be able to prepare full abstracts of common documentation.

The CG(C) must be able, in addition, to analyze evidence, to evaluate and, if necessary, verify information from secondary sources, to solve problems, and to prepare a proper family history. He must know thoroughly the bibliography, historiography, and terminology of his particular area of genealogical research.

Certificate holders are known as Associates of the Genealogical Institute of the Maritimes. A list of associates is provided to major documentary repositories, to associates and friends of the Institute, and upon request to members of the public. The list includes the names of all associates, and the mailing addresses of all those associates available to conduct paid research. Succinct descriptions of the expertise of the latter are also included.

A Friend of the Genealogical Institute of the Maritimes is an organization, or an individual other than an associate, who donates annually to the Institute a minimum of twenty dollars.

4. *Procedures*

To initiate his or her candidacy, an applicant is required to mail a preliminary application form, accompanied by the appropriate fee, to the Registrar of the Institute.

If the candidate's credentials appear adequate, the Registrar will request that he or she submit three unsigned copies of an appropriate sample of his or her work, accompanied by payment of the proper fee for the certification sought. The three copies will be given a number and assigned to readers. If the sample is found inadequate, the candidate may submit a second specimen of his or her work. An unsuccessful candidate for the CG(C) may alternatively at this point be invited to persist in his or her application, but for the GRS(C).

Following favourable reports from the readers, the candidate will be requested to appear for a two-hour written examination, followed by an oral interview. The CG(C) candidate must demonstrate a mastery of theory, methodology and records, while the GRS(C) will be tested on practical matters concerning record location and use. Examinations may be taken in various locations. All persons, whether resident in the Maritimes or from the exterior, must appear in person for this examination and interview.

Applications, work samples, and examinations may be in either English or French, at the election of the candidate.

The average time required to pass through the entire evaluation process, from submission of preliminary application to receipt of certificate, is twelve months.

Address

Requests for application forms and the current schedule of fees, as well as other correspondence, may be sent to

> The Registrar
> Genealogical Institute of the Maritimes
> P.O. Box 3142
> Halifax, N.S.
> B3J 3H5

Centre d'Etudes acadiennes

HISTORICAL OVERVIEW

For genealogical purposes, Acadian history may be divided into four distinct periods: (1) French colonization (1636-1713); (2) development under British rule (1713-1755); (3) deportation and dispersion (1755-1785); and (4) resettlement (after 1785). The various circumstances and events that produced the tragedy and hardships of the third of these periods affected directly the maintenance and survival of important groups of records.

For the period of colonization few records survive, due chiefly to numerous attacks by one or the other colonial rivals who fought over a territory so strategically important. All but a handful of the notarial records at Port-Royal, for example, were lost in a fire resulting from a British bombardment in 1710 (AN, G5, vol. 52, pièces 1, 2, 4-5). Similarly, at various other junctures many church registers were destroyed, leaving little extant material relevant to the histories of the colony's earliest families, particularly their European origins. Indeed, were it not for the large number of census records preserved in France, little could be done to reconstruct the first several generations of Acadian colonists.

During the decades of attempted neutrality under the British, more church records were produced that survive to this day, but few notarial archives were kept and none have been preserved, and no genealogically useful census materials were generated either. In sharp contrast is the rich documentation available for the islands retained by the French after the Treaty of Utrecht, particularly that concerning the fortress-city of Louisbourg.

Between 1755 and 1763 the dissolution of Acadian institutions and the eradication of Acadian settlements introduced a period of very sparse documentation. Yet even as they scattered the Acadians left marks of their passage in an astonishing array of lists, preserving the memory of their years as prisoners of war in Great Britain and the British colonies of North America or as refugees in France, the Antilles, South America, Louisiana, and Saint-Pierre and Miquelon. Apart from a handful of missionary registers, before 1785 there are few other sources for Acadians of Atlantic Canada. In many of the lands of exile, particularly France, Québec, and Louisiana, however, information abounds. Fortunate is the researcher whose quarry are found in one or other of those places and only returned to the Atlantic region very near or after the end of the eighteenth century.

The resettlement of the Acadians was slow and arduous. Thinly scattered along the Atlantic littoral, they began to move from squatter to landowner status in 1772. Parochial reorganization took years longer, beginning only in the 1780s. Of the parishes whose foundation predates 1800, few have all their registers, and several (e.g., Arichat, Church Point, and Memramcook) are missing substantial portions of them due to fires and other disasters.

More recently, apart from religious documentation, tracing Acadian families is much like tracing other groups; the same census materials and land and probate records often permit a thorough genealogical compilation. One particular distinction may be noted here, however. Whether unwilling or unable, few Acadian families invested in long-lasting funereal monuments. Thus Acadian cemeteries are less significant sources than might otherwise be expected, at least until the late nineteenth century.

MAJOR ARCHIVES

The foremost repository of Acadian archival material is the Centre d'Études acadiennes, Université de Moncton, Moncton, N.B. E1A 3E9. Created by Father Clément Cormier, c.s.c., in 1968, the Centre has a specialized library of 9,000 titles and an extensive manuscript collection. Everything available concerning the history of the Acadians through the first three periods mentioned above, and everything concerning those Acadians who remained in, or returned to, the Atlantic region after 1785, is collected here.

From its inception the Centre has had on staff a full-time genealogist who supervises the arrangement and classification of its genealogical material, consults with visiting researchers and correspondents, and compiles information for a compendium of Acadian genealogy (the *Dictionnaire généalogique des familles acadiennes*).

Genealogical material at the Centre d'Études acadiennes consists of both primary and secondary sources. Primary sources in its collections are principally copies of parish registers, notarial records, census reports, and assorted lists of Acadians in exile. The Centre has, for example, copies of all known pre-dispersion registers and registers of nearly all Acadian parishes of the Atlantic Provinces (except for a few areas of central and eastern Nova Scotia and western Newfoundland), at least down to 1900. These registers are greatly supplemented by the Centre's collection of census reports from 1671 to 1891. In addition to numerous genealogical publications, the Centre also possesses manuscripts of great value, including the notes of Placide Gaudet, Auguste-E. Daigle, Mgr. Louis Richard,

Rev. Archange Godbout, Rev. Hector Hébert, and Rev. Patrice Gallant. Further details regarding the Centre's holdings may be obtained from its *Inventaire général des sources documentaires sur les Acadiens*, tome 1 (Moncton, 1975), pp. 54-57, 380-469.

The Centre has published two volumes of genealogical importance: *Les Acadiens de Saint-Pierre & Miquelon à La Rochelle, 1767 à 1768 et 1778 à 1785* in 1977 and *Registre de l'abbé Charles-François Bailly (Caraquet), 1768 à 1773* in 1978. Additionally, the Centre's semi-annual bulletin, *Contact-Acadie*, contains reports regarding its genealogical sector and includes in each issue a brief article featuring new discoveries.

The *Dictionnaire généalogique des familles acadiennes* is intended to be a definitive work on Acadian genealogy, presenting all the information available from primary sources, while including references to the best secondary material. The first part of this work, to appear in two volumes, covers 1636 to 1714 and will be followed by a much larger section extending the family histories to 1780.

None of the Centre's material circulates. Consultation must be at the Centre, during its opening hours, weekdays 8:30-12:00 and 13:00-16:30. Photocopying is available. A limited amount of information may also be obtained through correspondence.

Extensive materials regarding Acadian genealogy were collected at the National (formerly Public) Archives of Canada during Placide Gaudet's employment there. These include transcriptions of many church records, original census materials, and a major portion of Gaudet's own notes. All of these materials are available on microfilm through interlibrary loan from the archives, 395 Wellington Street, Ottawa, Ontario K1A 0N3.

Other materials useful to Acadian research, particularly concerning the period of resettlement (after 1785), are available at the archives of each of the four Atlantic Provinces, and in local or regional Acadian archives such as the Centre acadien, Université Saint-Anne, Pointe-de-l'Église, N.S. B0W 1M0; Les Trois Pignons, C.P. 430, Chéticamp, N.S. B0E 1H0; and the Centre de documentation de la Société historique Nicolas-Denys, Centre universitaire de Shippagan, Shippagan, N.B. E0B 2P0.

VITAL RECORDS

For Acadians these are generally co-extensive with the records of the Catholic Church, discussed below.

Beginning in the mid-nineteenth century the same civil records of births, marriages, and deaths are available for Acadians as for other ethnic groups in the respective provinces.

CENSUS RECORDS

For the period of Acadia's colonization, these are the principal source of genealogical knowledge. Fortunately the French authorities required frequent nominal enumerations of the resident population. These occurred with greater frequency than most contemporary head-counts, at least during the last decades of French rule, between the Treaties of Breda (1667) and Utrecht (1713). Specifically, censuses were taken in 1671, 1678, 1686, 1693, 1695 (partial), 1698, c1700, 1701 (partially nominal), 1703 (heads of families), 1707 (heads of families), and 1714 (partially nominal). All but the enumeration of 1678 are in the Archives nationales de France, Colonies section, series G1, vol. 466. The 1678 census has been preserved among the Le Neuf papers in series E of the same archives. Photographic copies of the originals are available in Moncton and Ottawa. Additionally, transcriptions have been published in many places, notably in Father Donald Hébert, *Acadians in Exile* (Cecilia, Louisiana: Hébert Publications, 1980), pp. 456-553 (1671, 1686, 1714), and in the *Mémoires de la Société généalogique canadienne-française (SGCF)*, vol. 22 (1971), pp. 226-247 (1678). Plaisance (Placentia, Nfld.) has a similar series of censuses (1671, 1673, 1691, 1693, 1694, 1698, c1700, 1704, 1706, 1711), the originals of which are also in series G1 (vol. 467). Only the first two of these are nominal. All have been published in SGCF, vol. 10 (1959), pp. 179-188; vol. 11 (1960), pp. 69-85; and vol. 13 (1962), pp. 204-208, 244-255.

The only enumeration of genealogical value for all of British Acadia during the period 1713-1755 is Winslow's list, preserved in the Massachusetts Historical Society, and transcribed in the *Collections of the Nova Scotia Historical Society*, vol. 3 (1883), pp. 114-123. By contrast many heads of families censuses were taken in Ile Royale (C.B.) (1713, 1715, 1716, 1717, c1720, 1724, 1726, 1734) and Ile Saint-Jean (P.E.I.) (1728, 1730, 1734, 1735) prior to the marvelously detailed, nominal *voyage d'inspection* of the Sieur de La Roque in 1752. There is also a nominal census of Ile Royale of 1749. All these censuses are found in series G1 of the Archives des colonies, vol. 466, and copies are available in Moncton and Ottawa. La Roque's census has been published in the *Report Concerning Canadian Archives for the Year 1905*, Vol. 2 (Ottawa, 1906), App. A, Pt. 1.

The principal enumerations of Acadians during the years of exile include (1) those appended to the requests of the Acadians in the British colonies to be repatriated in 1763 (in the Archives nationales, Affaires étrangères section, Angleterre, vol. 450-451, published in J.-E. Roy, *Rapport sur les Archives de France* (Ottawa, 1911), pp. 617-647), (2) those included in the La Rochette papers of the same year (in the National Archives of Canada, MG 18, vol. 1, f. 14, published in Rieder & Rieder, *The Acadians in France*, vol. 2 (Metairie, Louisiana, 1972), pp. 85-121), and (3) the annual *rôles* of the former inhabitants of Ile Royale and Ile Saint-Jean in Brittany and Normandy between 1762 and 1773 (in series G1 of the Archives des colonies, vol. 482-483, those of 1762 and 1772 published in Rieder & Rieder, *The Acadians in France*, vol. 1 [Metairie, Louisiana, 1967]). In the Atlantic region itself, only Saint-Pierre and Miquelon had frequent censuses (1767, 1776, 1785), the originals of which are again in series G1, vol. 458, 463, and 467. These censuses have been published in Michel Poirier, *Les Acadiens aux îles Saint-Pierre et Miquelon* (Moncton, 1984), pp. 201-218, 261-295, 360-374, with the exception of the Saint-Pierre section of the last of them. For more detail regarding censuses and lists of this period and later, see *Inventaire général des sources documentaires sur les Acadiens*, tome 1, pp. 413-423, 437-469.

After 1785 little census material concerning the Acadians is available before the provincial censuses of 1827 and 1838 (N.S.), 1841 (P.E.I.), 1851 (N.B.), and 1861 (N.S. and N.B.), and the federal censuses of 1871, 1881, and 1891. A nominal census of Chéticamp and Margaree, dating from 1809, in the archives of the Archdiocese of Québec (N.-E., VII-22, published in Rev. Anselme Chiasson, *Chéticamp* [Moncton, 1972], pp. 291-295), and partial heads of families enumerations of Cape Breton Island in 1811 and 1818 (published in D.C. Harvey, comp., *Holland's Description of Cape Breton Island* [Halifax, 1935], pp. 136-168) are invaluable aids to research in those areas. See also the materials described in the just-cited section of *Inventaire général des sources documentaires sur les Acadiens*.

LAND AND PROBATE RECORDS

For the Acadians under the French Regime, these documents were kept in the notarial archives, along with marriage contracts, *donations entre vifs*, sales of sailing vessels, apprenticeships, powers of attorney, and all manner of other business documents. Unfortunately, as has already been mentioned, very few notarial records still exist for peninsular Acadia. There are a small portion of the minutes of Jean-Chrysostôme Loppinot in series G3 of the Colonies section of the Archives nationales (de France), carton 2040. A selection of these materials was abstracted and published in the *Mémoires de la Société généalogique canadienne-française*, vol. 5 (1952-1953), pp. 38-41. Copies are also available at Moncton and Ottawa.

The extent to which the notarial archives may be useful for genealogical research is clearly shown by the richness of those that still exist for Plaisance (1697-1714) and Louisbourg (1715- 1758). The originals of these are also in series G3, cartons 7/175, 8/176, 2037-2039, 2041-2047, 2055-2058. Copies are available at Moncton and Ottawa. The marriage contracts in cartons 2037-2047 and 2055-2058 have been abstracted in Rev. Donald Hébert, *Acadians in Exile* (Cecilia, Louisiana, 1980).

No comparable documentation exists for any of the Acadians of the Atlantic region after 1758, except for those who resided at Saint-Pierre and Miquelon. These materials are in series G3, carton 478. The marriage contracts from this collection have also been abstracted in Father Hébert's *Acadians in Exile*.

As for other ethnic groups, and beginning with the first grants to Acadians in Nova Scotia in 1772, much information may be obtained from the land and probate registries in the respective counties of the Atlantic Provinces. The Centre d'Études acadiennes has copies or extracts of selected Acadian land petitions in various parts of New Brunswick and Nova Scotia, particularly Cape Breton, as well as microfilms of the deeds of Westmorland County, N.B. (1785-1899).

CHURCH RECORDS

Where they are reasonably intact and were well kept, the registers of baptisms, marriages, and burials of the Catholic Church are the principal source for research in Acadian genealogy. Unfortunately, for the period of Acadia's colonization very few registers survive. A small register of Beaubassin's records covering 1679 to 1686 is in the archives of the Archdiocese of Québec, and was transcribed in Winston DeVille's *Acadian Church Records* (New Orleans, 1975), pp. 2-9. The extant registers of Port-Royal begin in 1702 and those of Grand-Pré in 1707. Beaubassin recommences in 1712.

It is only for the second period of Acadia's history that the church records of its principal parishes are reasonably continuous. The original registers of Port-Royal are at the Public Archives of Nova Scotia (1702-1728) and in the archives of the Diocese of Yarmouth, N.S. (1727-1755). The Rieder family has transcribed and published these records, to 1740, as volumes 3-5 of *Acadian Church Records* (Metairie, Louisiana, 1977-1984). Grand-Pré's registers (1707-1748) are in the archives of the Diocese of Baton Rouge, Louisiana. The diocese published a transcription of this data in volume I of its *Catholic Church Records* (1978), pp. 1-135.

Beaubassin's registers (1712-1723, 1732-1735, 1740-1748) are in the Archives départementales de la Charente-Maritime in La Rochelle, France. The Rieders also published a transcription of these registers as volume 2 of their *Acadian Church Records* (Metairie, Louisiana, 1976). Another small register from Chipoudy and Petitcoudiac (1753-1757) is also in the archives of the Archdiocese of Québec. A transcription was included in DeVille's *Acadian Church Records* just mentioned, pp. 10-22. The registers of other parishes, at Cobeguit, Pisiguit (two), Rivière-aux-Canards, another parish at Port-Royal (St. Laurent), Chébogue, Pointe-de-Beauséjour, and Pays-Bas, were all lost at the time of the Acadian dispersion.

No registers of Plaisance survive, but Ile Royale and Ile Saint-Jean have records from as early as 1714. The registers of Louisbourg (1722-1745, 1749-1758), Port-Lajoie (1721-1744, 1749- 1758), La Baleine and Lorembec (1714-1745, 1750-1757), Saint- Esprit (1726-1745, 1749), and Port-aux-Basques (Nfld.) (1740) comprise volumes 406-411 in series G1 of the Colonies section of the Archives nationales (de France). The Registers of St. Pierre-du-Nord (1724-1745, 1749-1758) are in the Archives départementales d'Ille-et-Vilaine, at Rennes, France. Copies of all of these are available in Moncton and Ottawa, but none has been published. As in peninsular Acadia, the registers of other parishes (Port-Toulouse, Petit-de-Grat, and Port-Dauphin in Ile Royale, Malpèque, Rivière-du-Nord-Est, and Pointe-Prime in Ile Saint-Jean) were lost at the time of the evacuations of 1758, or after-wards in France.

The year 1758 marked the end of parochial organization for Acadians in the Atlantic region. Until the establishment of new parishes beginning in the 1780s, the only records are those found in the missionary registers of Fathers C.-F. Bailly and J.-M. Bourg. Bailly left two registers, one at Kingsclear, N.B. (1767-1768), and one at Caraquet (1768-1773). The latter, as already noted, was transcribed and published by the Centre d'Études acadiennes in 1978. Copies of both are in the Centre. The originals were long kept in their separate parishes, but the Caraquet register is now in the diocesan archives at Bathurst, and the Kingsclear register at Saint-Basile, N.B. The register of Sainte-Anne de Restigouche (1759-1761) and Father Bourg's register of Carleton (1773-1795) found their way into the Archives judiciaires at Québec. Photographic copies are at Restigouche and Moncton.

Registers of modern parishes should ordinarily be complete, but fires and other disasters have left substantial gaps in many areas. The registers of the Dioceses of Bathurst, Edmundston, and Saint John in N.B., of Charlottetown in P.E.I., and of the Archdiocese of Halifax in N.S. have all been microfilmed by the Genealogical Society of the Church of Jesus Christ of Latter-day Saints (the Mormons). Copies of the microfilms of the Dioceses of Bathurst to 1920, Edmundston to 1920, and Charlottetown to 1900, are held at the Centre d'Études acadiennes and elsewhere. The Centre also has microfilm copies of the registers of the Archdiocese of Moncton, N.B. to 1910, and the Diocese of Yarmouth, N.S. to 1910, as well as photocopies of selected early nineteenth century registers for Arichat, Chéticamp, D'Escousse, Havre-Boucher, Margaree, Pomquet, and Tracadie in the Diocese of Antigonish, and for Chezzetcook and Menoudie in the Archdiocese of Halifax.

CEMETERY RECORDS

Cemeteries are generally not a fruitful source of information for Acadian research until the late 1800s. It was long customary in Acadian communities to mark the final resting place of loved ones with simple wooden crosses which have long since disappeared. The graveyards of the first three periods of Acadian history, to 1785, bear no individual markers today at all. In some areas stone markers date to the 1820s, but these are uncommon. Substantial numbers of gravestones are found only from about the 1870s.

Burial information was regularly entered in Catholic Church registers, discussed above.

In recent years much interest has been raised in transcribing information from grave markers of older cemeteries. A number of Acadian parishes have been copied, including Amherst, Arichat, Chéticamp, Chezzetcook, East Pubnico, Joggins, and Menoudie, N.S., and Souris, P.E.I., transcriptions for all of which are at Moncton. An alphabetized version of the Arichat transcription by Merrill F. Boudreau appeared in *The Nova Scotia Genealogist*, Vol. 2 (1984), pp. 26-29. Other transcriptions may be found at local historical repositories.

IMMIGRATION

Apart from their eighteenth century dispersion, immigration patterns for Acadians have been similar to those for other groups. The second half of the nineteenth century witnessed a large-scale movement to New England, especially to eastern Massachusetts, although some of the more adventurous migrated to all corners of the continent, even to the Pacific coast, or settled in the Old World. Distinctive patterns of settlement emerged almost at once in the New England areas where these people concentrated. Old neighbours from the Atlantic Provinces often became neighbours again in the working-class communities near New England's fisheries or mills. For an analysis of a small, but typical, part of this flow of immigration see the writer's "The Arichat Frenchmen in Gloucester," *New England Historical and Genealogical Register*, vol. 131 (1977), pp. 83-99.

NEWSPAPERS

In his article "État des recherches sur la presse française en Acadie," *Cahiers de la Société historique acadienne,* vol. 6 (1975), pp. 25-42, Roger Lacerte lists thirty-three Acadian newspapers that were published between the 1860s and 1972. Many of these did not long survive, but several, including *Le Moniteur Acadien* (1867-1926), *Le Courrier des Provinces Maritimes,* (1885-1901), *L'Évangéline* (1887-1982), and *L'Impartial* (1893-1915), were influential papers with wide circulations. All four carried announcements of births, marriages, and deaths, and as the Acadian renaissance progressed all included in their pages articles of historical or genealogical character, often written by the celebrated genealogist Placide Gaudet. *L'Impartial* even published a special issue on the occasion of the centennial of Tignish, P.E.I. (1900), which included genealogical tables of the Acadian families of the parish. The Centre d'Études acadiennes possesses copies of all these papers. Additionally, inventories have been prepared for all four, permitting ready access to all substantial articles. The vital statistics in these newspapers, except those in *L'Impartial,* have yet to be catalogued or indexed.

The limited Acadian material in the English press has been slowly emerging with publication of the "Vital Statistics from Newspapers" series in New Brunswick (1784-1870) and Nova Scotia (1769-1854). These series are continuing, and more recent newspapers will be added to those already culled.

SPECIAL SOURCES

Besides materials outlined in the preceding sections, Acadian researchers have several special sources available to help them. First in importance among these is something commonly called the *Déclarations de Belle-île-en-Mer.* In order to qualify for land in a colonization project on Belle-île, off the Breton coast, over seventy-five heads of families were obliged to depose all they knew of their ancestry, back to their first forebears who immigrated to Acadia from France. Many relationships not otherwise clear and many dates are supplied in these depositions, especially for the families of l'Assomption parish in Pisiguit. The *Déclarations* were first transcribed in the *Collection de documents inédits sur le Canada et l'Amérique* published by *Le Canada-français* (Québec, 1889-1890), vol. 2, pp. 165-194, vol. 3, pp. 5-134, but only the more recent Rieder & Rieder transcription in *The Acadians in France,* vol. 2 (Metairie, Louisiana, 1972), is indexed. The originals are in each of the parishes at Belle- île.

A second important special source is the series of petitions which Acadians wishing to marry had to present to ecclesiastical authorities in Louisiana in order to obtain dispensation from impediments of consanguinity or affinity. Petitioners were required to explain fully the relationships between prospective spouses. The original petitions, in Spanish, are in the archives of Notre Dame University in Indiana. Copies are held at Moncton. An indexed English language abstract of the whole collection was published by Shirley Bourquard as *Marriage Dispensations in the Diocese of Louisiana and the Floridas: 1786-1803* (New Orleans, 1980).

Finally, among special sources are the lists of Acadians arriving in the port of Saint-Servan. These lists include the names of not only the great majority of Acadians deported from Ile Saint-Jean and Ile Royale in 1758, but also all those who died during the crossing. Many relationships not revealed elsewhere are established here. The original lists are in the Archives de la Marine at Brest. An indexed transcription was published by Rieder & Rieder as volume 3 of *The Acadians in France* (Metairie, Louisiana, 1973).

SOCIETIES

There are no Acadian genealogical societies in the Atlantic Provinces, although there are numerous Acadian historical societies, including the following:

Société historique acadienne
C.P. 2363, Succursale A
Moncton, N.B.
E1C 8J3

Société historique Nicolas-Denys
Centre universitaire
Shippagan, N.B.
E0B 2P0

Société d'histoire de la rivière Saint-Jean
715 Priestman
Fredericton, N.B.
E3B 5W7

Société historique acadienne de la Baie Saint-Marie
Université Sainte-Anne
Pointe-de-l'Église, N.S.
B0W 1M0

Société historique acadienne de Pubnico-Ouest
Pubnico-Ouest le Centre, Yarmouth County
N.S.
B0W 2M0

Société historique acadienne de l'île Madame
Arichat, Richmond County
N.S.
B0E 1A0

Société Saint-Pierre
Les Trois Pignons
C.P. 430
Chéticamp, N.S.
B0E 1H0

Société historique acadienne de l'île-du-Prince-Edouard
C.P. 88
Summerside, P.E.I.
C1N 4P6

PERIODICALS

There are two Acadian genealogical periodicals in the United States that include material of interest:

Acadian Genealogy Exchange
863 Wayman Branch Road
Covington, Kentucky 41015

Le Reveil Acadien
P.O. Box 53
Marlborough, Massachusetts 01752

BIBLIOGRAPHY

a. Centre d'Études acadiennes, *Inventaire général des sources documentaires sur les Acadiens*, tome 1 (Moncton: Editions d'Acadie, 1975).

b. Roger Comeau, *Guide des sources de l'histoire acadienne aux Archives publiques du Canada* (Ottawa: Public Archives of Canada, 1962).

c. Genealogical Department, Church of Jesus Christ of Latter-day Saints, *Major Record Sources for Acadian Genealogical Research* (reprinted in the *Cahiers de la Société historique acadienne*, vol. 3 (1970), pp. 373-384).

d. Rev. Donald J. Hébert, *Acadians in Exile* (Cecilia, LA: Hébert Publications, 1980), appendices I-V, pp. 443-710).

INDEX OF SUBJECTS AND INSTITUTIONS

POSTSCRIPT BY THE PUBLISHER

In October 1986 the William H. Donner Foundation, Inc. of New York City awarded the New England Historic Genealogical Society (NEHGS), 101 Newbury Street, Boston, MA 02116, a two-year grant of $50,000 to acquire Canadian genealogical materials, mostly books and microforms. This splendid gift has allowed NEHGS to become, we hope, the major center in the eastern United States for Canadian and Canadian-American genealogy. Americans with Canadian ancestry are thus invited to visit the Society before travelling, or en route, to New Brunswick, Newfoundland and Labrador, Nova Scotia, or Prince Edward Island, and Atlantic Canadians coming to the United States are invited to pursue their genealogical interests here as well.

Major new Canadian acquisitions at NEHGS include (some on many microfiches or rolls of microfilm):

1. All extant Canadian censuses through 1891. (NEHGS will acquire the 1901 census in January, 1993.)

2. All published New Brunswick census, marriage and newspaper vital statistics volumes.

3. All filmed Nova Scotia marriage bonds and licenses; all filmed extant Nova Scotia births and deaths 1864-77, and marriages 1864-1918; all filmed township books.

4. P.E.I. Master Name Index; all filmed Roman Catholic and many Protestant P.E.I. church records; all filmed P.E.I. marriage licenses and bonds, plus all filmed justice of the peace marriage registers; filmed extracts of pre-1886 (for deaths and burials pre-1907) church vital records; filmed copybooks of P.E.I. wills through 1900.

5. All major published source materials on the Acadians, both in Atlantic Canada and Louisiana.

6. Loiselle marriage index (of 540 mostly Quebec parishes); all filmed Quebec church records, both Catholic and Protestant, to 1880; many filmed Quebec notarial records; filmed and indexed Lower Canada land papers (including depositions, petitions, and other legal documents) through 1841; and many published works, including René Jetté, *Dictionnaire généalogique des familles du Québec des origines à 1730* and *Répertoires des actes de baptême, mariage, sépulture et des recensements du Québec ancien*, 40 volumes to date (Quebec church vital records, all through 1749, many through 1765).

7. Some cemetery and other records for Ontario and western Canada.